POV Press
Books by Bethanne Kim

The Constitution: It's the OS for the US

Not the Zombies:
> *#1: OMG!*
> *#2: BRB!*
> *#3: YOLO!*

The Organized Wedding: Planning Everything from Your Engagement to Your Marriage

Scouting in the Deep End:
> *#1: Cubmastering: Getting Started as Cubmaster*
> *#2: Scout Leader: An Introduction to Boy Scouts*
> *#3: Citizenship in the World: Teaching the Merit Badge*

Survival Skills for All Ages:
> *#1: 26 Basic Life Skills*
> *#2: 26 Mental & Urban Life Skills*
> *#3: Simple Cooking for Families*
> *#4: Simple Cooking for Allergies: OAS and Low Histamine Food*

Forthcoming:

Scouting in the Deep End:
> *Association with Adults*

Survival Skills for All Ages:
> *26 Outdoor Life Skills*
> *Special Needs Prepping*

SIMPLE COOKING FOR ALLERGIES: OAS AND LOW HISTAMINE FOOD

BETHANNE KIM

1. Cookbooks–Allergies
2. Cookbooks–General

eBook ISBN: 978-1-942533-26-9
Paperback ISBN: 978-1-942533-25-2

Distributed by POV Press
PO Box 399
Catharpin, VA 20143

Printed in the United States of America

DEDICATION

For Roberta, Kim, and all my mommy friends who have to deal with massive allergy and food issues with their own families and who have been a sounding board and help for me with my own food and allergy issues.

For Dr. Blaire, who is an outstanding allergist and a generally nice human being. She has made a huge difference in my life.

And of course, for my loving and supportive family, who have had their diets completely upended by my dietary issues. On the plus side, I have been baking from scratch for them a lot more.

TABLE OF CONTENTS

TABLE OF CONTENTS

TABLE OF CONTENTS

TABLE OF CONTENTS

TABLE OF CONTENTS

TABLE OF CONTENTS

TABLE OF CONTENTS

INTRODUCTION

I am writing this because I need food and recipes, and by putting it into a cookbook, I can help others. Cooking has definitely not been a life-long hobby. My friends tell me that the logical thing for most people would be to collect recipes in a folder. They were amused that (for me) the logical thing to do was to write and publish a cookbook. And, for me, the natural place to start was with online research to understand not just what I could/couldn't eat but why.

The first few chapters are a summary of what I learned. **The most important point: This is a fuzzy area without a lot of definitive research. Every effort has been made to ensure information is accurate, but this is only a starting point for your own research and conversations with your doctor.** That's where I started, and it's where everyone should start.

The recipe choices are idiosyncratic. They are things I wanted, my family wanted, or I thought a lot of people would like. I modified a deviled egg recipe because I like deviled eggs, and the same for the peanut soup. I went in search of sauces to replace tomato sauce instead of just using olive oil because one of my kids refuses to eat olive oil. I added a section on holidays when my family struggled with what to eat. In a few cases, I included recipes shared on social media. I don't like cooking. I'm not an accomplished cook, and I'm not patient enough to spend a long time in the kitchen or use a ton of ingredients. These recipes reflect that. They are (mostly) simple. They are easily adapted. And they don't take a lot of skill. As I worked on this cookbook, I added recipes and chapters when I felt my diet lacked something, like sauce to use as marinade and for chicken strips.

Most recipes in this book note the website or book where I found them. They have been modified to some degree, most often by changing or removing spices, to make them compliant or close to it for an OAS/low histamine diet. Some are from my recipe box. The variety of sites isn't because I was unable to find a variety of recipes at a single site, it's because I avoided using the same sites repeatedly. My goal is to give you an idea of how many places have potential, once you understand how histamine in food can impact you, and to encourage you to check out some of those sites.

Your individual sensitivities may require tweaking these recipes still farther (mine do—I'm allergic to garlic and onions) but the emphasis is on simplifying recipes so you can eliminate as many problematic foods as possible. Recipes also note options for changing or adding ingredients as you move away from a strict elimination diet. As you become comfortable with what you can and can't do within these restrictions, you can (hopefully) modify your own favorite meals to fit.

It's very important to understand that this isn't a diet in the way Paleo, Atkins, or others are. You can't just eliminate all the foods on these lists for long and still be healthy, which is part of the reason for taking a somewhat flexible approach in some of the recipes. If your doctor recommends following a strict low-histamine and OAS diet for a few weeks as an elimination diet, that's fine and this book can help you do that, but **don't just launch into an elimination diet without your doctor or nutritionist's involvement.** With that said, long-term changes can certainly be safely made to replace some foods with lower histamine options, such as replacing tomato sauce with olive oil, and continue following the basic guidelines.

These recipes can be part of a longer-term modification of your diet. For example, I can eat some restaurant chicken tenders but sauces are extremely dicey for me, so I make my own sauces.

When I first read all my OAS/low histamine restrictions, I wailed, "If it tastes like food and you enjoy it, I can't have it!" After researching and writing this book, I no longer feel that way. I discovered that I really do have choices, including foods I genuinely enjoy. I sought our recipes not just for my favorite but for widely popular foods like meatloaf and matzo ball soup so I could present an eclectic array of "normal" recipes to help you see the possibilities and inspire you to both modify your own favorites and to find new favorites.

In the final analysis, I'm just a woman with a lot of allergy issues, not a nutritionist, medical professional, or trained specialist. Please remember that this is <u>in no way</u> being presented as balanced nutrition or any kind of solution for allergies or anything else. You need to listen to your own body and your doctor. What works for one person won't 100% work for others, especially with histamine issues.

Good luck and happy eating!

Bethanne Kim

P.S. I wrote these recipes a little differently. Instead of one long list of ingredients at the beginning, the ingredients are split up throughout the recipe to (hopefully) make it easier to see when and where to add each one.

1. MY STORY

I have a ton of environmental allergies including a mold allergy that spun completely out of control when we had 300% of our normal rainfall one summer. Nothing ever got a chance to dry out. Garlic is an anti-fungal and may help some people with mold allergies. I was feeling desperate and decided to try a garlic capsule as a bit of a Hail Mary.

That was around 1:00 pm on Labor Day and it changed my life.

Most allergies can be associated a histamine response but not all allergies all cause a reaction (hives, nausea, etc.) beyond that. I was slightly allergic to onions and garlic. Even a tiny amount of onion made me nauseous but I had no noticeable reaction to garlic. Cooking onions (like many fruits and vegetables) breaks down proteins that cause a reaction so I didn't think garlic powder would cause a problem, especially since I never noticed a reaction to garlic. Unknown to me, the garlic was apparently dehydrated, not cooked, and that is a critical difference.

Three minutes after I took the garlic capsule, my hands started shaking and I felt like a freight train had smashed into me. My heart was pounding like I was running for my life even though I was relaxing on the sofa, chatting. That garlic capsule triggered symptoms that continued until about 6:00 am the next morning. If you're looking back to do the math, that's 17 hours of a racing heart/palpitations and other unpleasantness, plus other side effects that continued until my system finally calmed down days later.

While my body was still desperately trying to recover, I unthinkingly ate a piece of pizza with garlic in the sauce and my body went back on alert. I started getting hives when I ate food I had eaten freely in the past. And by "in the past," I mean the previous weekend. My allergist is a lovely woman who saw me right away and immediately put me on an oral allergy syndrome (OAS) and low histamine diet. Within two weeks, this diet, with an assist from antihistamines, had me feeling better than I had in months. It was amazing!

What wasn't amazing was my diet. I was subsisting on saltines, yogurt, applesauce, noodles with no sauce, and chicken breasts with olive oil and rosemary. The chicken was tasty but…boring. Part of the problem was that I had been reacting to so many things I was terrified to eat anything else until I absolutely knew my system had calmed down. My diet was bland, boring, and I couldn't wait to start adding more food. My doctor was so pleased with how much I improved she told me to stay on it and add new foods one at a time. For my part, I wanted a way to keep the benefits of this diet while remaining healthy (remember: a strict elimination diet isn't healthy long-term) and add more foods (now that it felt safe) so I could actually enjoy eating again. Clearly, I needed more options but I was afraid to eat anything not on the lists as compliant and I couldn't find anything to help me with the combination of OAS and low histamine diets.

Now that I was ready to try adding more food, the first thing I did was start researching to really understand what I could and couldn't eat, and why. Eliminating all the foods on every low-histamine list is not realistic, especially combined with an OAS diet, so I wanted to know which foods caused the biggest problems and why different foods cause problems. The most important thing I learned is that there haven't been enough studies to know conclusively how different foods impact people. Your doctor may recommend using this as an elimination diet to help you learn your dietary triggers, which should help you, but don't do any elimination diet without talking to your doctor first and as you go through the process.

I learned to read all my food labels. I also learned that I react after about three minutes to truly problematic foods, so I eat a bite or two of new foods, then wait about three minutes before continuing. (Three minutes is my threshold, you need to figure out how your body responds.) I also learned the combination of anti-histamines that stops my reactions. If I feel like I am stressing my body out by eating non-compliant foods, I stop and go back to foods I know are "safe" until my body calms down again. It usually takes a meal or two of saltines, cottage cheese, and toast, then I'm okay again.

This diet has changed my life but ultimately not in a bad way, despite a few rough weeks in the beginning. Being allergic to garlic creates a lot of barriers to eating anything pre-cooked from the grocery store or at restaurants and I can't spin that as a positive but at least I know. That is an allergy issue, though, not a histamine issue. I had struggled to sleep a full night without needing my asthma rescue inhaler. Now, I can not only sleep all night but I can breathe deeply, truly filling my lungs for the first time in too many months.

In my case, I believe that some food choices I made trying to be healthy backfired. I also had almost-constant exposure to garlic and garlic powder (it's in everything), causing my body to constantly release histamine to fight it. My body simply had far, far more histamine than it could possibly handle. This diet helped battle my histamines back to a level it could handle. Since I have to cook a lot from scratch to avoid garlic, it makes sense to continue following low histamine guidelines for a large portion of my meals. After all, it's no more work to use ground chicken than ground beef, and chicken is compliant, beef isn't. Allergy shots are helping, and hopefully in a few years I will be free of seasonal allergies, but why make my body struggle harder than it needs to?

For all the benefits this diet has given me, I still want to actually enjoy eating. The day I was excited because I could eat graham crackers and they seemed flavorful was the day I started seriously looking for compliant meals that don't suck. The final chapter of this book explains how I altered recipes to make them compliant so you can do the same for your favorite recipes.

As I work toward my new "normal", I am slowly adding foods back into my diet but in a thoughtful, not random, way. I love cinnamon and can eat it now, but it wasn't one of the first foods I tried because spices are definitely a problem for me. I try a new one every few months, when I'm feeling stable. Cinnamon was, however, one of the first spices I tried because I love it, and because it's super common. I don't know exactly where I'll end up, but I'm starting this journey by adding back the things that are most annoying to cut out and that I miss, like chocolate and cinnamon.

This book is the result of my search for meals I can enjoy with my family. It has taken me to a lot of websites and gotten me to try new foods and new cooking techniques. I have had to give up some things I truly love because the garlic simply can't be removed from them (garlic bread) but I have found other new-to-me foods I enjoy (matzo ball soup, Dutch baby). You will need to make your own choices about what you can tolerate for foods you truly love. I hope it inspires you!

2. How Does it Work?

Histamines are chemicals in your body's immune system that help it remove bothersome things like allergens. Ongoing high levels of histamine can create problems, including chronic inflammation, which is one reason to try to keep histamine levels under control. Since anti-histamines are commonly used for allergic reactions, the strongest association most people have for histamines is with allergies, and that is certainly one place they come into play.

Histamine in food is a relatively new area of study and scientists aren't 100% sure what foods are high in histamine or are histamine liberators. At least as importantly, they do know that those qualities vary tremendously within a food based on things like age, storage, preparation, additives, and more. On top of that, each person's body chemistry, personal allergens, and allergen response all have an impact. There are a lot of unknowns and very, very few knowns. This adds up to: <u>It's impossible to predict with 100% certainty how histamine in a specific food will impact your body and your allergies.</u>

Foods high in histamine are foods that naturally contain a lot of histamine, such as sausage, tomatoes, and spinach. Histamine liberators are things that free histamine from other sources. Both work to increase the total amount of histamine in your system, just in different ways. Some people also need to reduce or eliminate gluten, casein, soy, and "nightshades" (potatoes, paprika, tomatoes, spicy peppers) but your doctor can address those with you, if necessary. They aren't a focus in this book but since nightshades can be a histamine issue, there is a list of them in Appendix 4. You may want to look for recipes by searching for "nightshade free" options, such as nightshade free chili.

When my doctor gave me the twin lists of what to avoid for oral allergy syndrome (OAS) and a low histamine diet, I was totally and utterly overwhelmed. I felt like there was nothing I could eat and I didn't understand what I was trying to avoid. The truth is that if I had strictly avoided every single food on every single list, I might have been down to quinoa, brown rice, and hard-boiled egg yolks. Clearly, that's not healthy and it isn't something my doctor recommended.

<u>The information in this book is culled from what I received from my doctor and my own online research.</u> **I am not a doctor, nutritionist, or any sort of medical professional.**

The next two chapters in this book explain OAS and histamine in foods, continue with recommendations on getting started and general guidelines, then finally move on to the actual recipes. The Appendixes include food lists to note what you can and can't tolerate because it can get hard to remember what you have already cleared as okay or learned to avoid. Also, it's easier for others to prepare food for you if they have a list of what you can and can't eat. OAS and high histamine foods are noted in those lists. If you want to learn more, start with the articles in Appendix 1 and 2.

Oral Allergy Syndrome (OAS)

If you have seasonal allergies to one thing (e.g., ragweed pollen) and eat something related to it (e.g., bananas, melons, cucumbers, zucchini), you may react to the related food even if you aren't actually allergic to it, especially when your pollen allergies are high. Your body gets confused since they are similar and it's on high alert.

Because OAS is triggered when specific allergen levels are high, following an OAS compliant diet can be seasonal and short-term (a few months of the year), but that depends on your circumstances and your doctor's recommendations. Fresh fruits and veggies are the main focus with OAS but many sites recommend avoiding peanuts, sunflower seeds, soybeans, lentils and certain spices as well, especially if tree pollen is an issue. Removing the skin may help if the problematic proteins are focused there, but it isn't a guarantee and doesn't work for everyone or every food.

The proteins that cause an OAS reaction are normally damaged or even destroyed by cooking, so they are generally (but not always, so use care) safe to eat when fully and completely cooked, but not uncooked or cooked al dente. For example, apples in applesauce and bananas in banana bread are fully, completely, and thoroughly cooked. Slow cooker (Crockpot™) cooking is a good way to ensure this. Boiling and pureeing can also be effective, opening up a lot of options for soup and sauce. **Cooking does not necessarily destroy problematic proteins in celery or spices.** If you react to celery or spices, be very mindful of reactions or avoid them entirely (Appendix 2: Specific Topics).

Histamine

For most people, histamine in food doesn't cause problems. For people sensitive to histamine, it can cause allergy-like problems and make true allergies worse. Some foods either release histamine or destabilize mast cells, leading to increased internal histamine levels. Mast cells are a part of your immune system that stores histamine.

High Histamine Foods

Proteins form when long chains of amino acids join together. As these proteins break down, they release the amines they are formed from, including histamine, tryptamine, and tyramine. **This is why freshness and following safe food handling (e.g., keeping food refrigerated.) is critical for a low histamine diet.**

Histamines occur naturally in many foods but this process of breaking down amino acids makes them accumulate as food ages and proteins begin to break down, which is why freshness is critical for fruits, veggies, and meat/poultry on a low-histamine diet. While a few days (or weeks) matters less for food with longer shelf-life, including cheese, it still matters. Aged cheeses such as cheddar, blue cheese, and anything labeled "aged" have much higher histamine levels than "young" cheeses such as ricotta, cream cheese, cottage cheese, mild cheddar, and young Gouda.

Histamine Liberating Foods

It's just like it sounds. These foods free (liberate) histamine from mast cells or basophils. Sadly, chocolate, strawberries, shellfish, and citrus fruits are all histamine liberating foods.

Histamine Lowering Foods

Yes, they exist! Some foods contain "quercetin" in abundance, notably apples, cucumbers, and onions, and quercetin helps lower histamine. Naturally, all three of those can create issues for those with OAS. Ironically, many foods that are high in quercetin are commonly found on low histamine "no" lists, which is a good illustration of how much remains under debate and how hard it is to pin down if specific foods are really good or bad for you.

Histamine lowering spices include nigella, ginger, turmeric, coriander, thyme, and garlic. (High-quercetin onions and garlic are closely related.) Coriander and thyme can be problematic for OAS.

Diamine oxidase (DAO)

Diamine oxidase (DAO) is believed to be the primary enzyme that breaks down ingested histamine (e.g., from food). DAO is stored in intestinal mucosa but needs to be released into the gut. Foods can block, aid, or be neutral in this process. If you don't have enough DAO available to break down the extra histamine in your body, it may keep building up, creating more and more problems.

DAO Blocking Foods

Alcohol, many kinds of tea, and energy drinks seem to block DAO to some degree. This is a new field and much is still unknown.

High DAO Foods

Very little has been learned yet about high DAO foods, but they do exist. Oleic acid, found in olive oil, has been shown to increase the release of DAO into the bloodstream up to five-fold. Poultry and lamb are also good sources of oleic acid as well as protein.

Legumes, especially chickpeas, soybeans, and lentils, are high DAO foods. Sprouting them increase their DAO. Legume seedlings have lots of DAO because baby plants use it to build stems and more. They are often categorized as high histamine and can be OAS triggers, but their other beneficial properties may balance that out, depending on the person and how their body is doing at that time. Overall, legumes are a mixed bag. In short, use care and don't eat a ton, but if you can eat them, include them when you can. Personally, I like roasted chickpeas as a quick snack.

Nightshades

"Deadly nightshade" is Belladonna, an ancient poison no one ingests on purpose. The more generic category of related fruits and vegetables contain elements that don't impact most people but can cause inflammation in sensitive people. Nightshades (members of the Solanaceae family) include potatoes, tomatoes, hot peppers, and quite a few popular spices. They are absolutely a potential histamine issue, so keep an eye on your reactions to them. See Appendix 4 for a list of nightshades.

Gut Health/Probiotics

The link between a healthy gut and healthy histamine levels isn't discussed a great deal because studies are still in their infancy but what I found was compelling. Certain histamine-creating gut bacteria can become overactive, leading to problems including an inability to process all the histamine in your food. Fermented foods, including pickles and yogurt, are particularly complicit in this because they can feed the exact bacteria that produce histamine.

HOW DOES IT WORK?

What does this mean in practical terms? If you think the bacteria in your gut may be out of balance, be especially careful to exclude fermented foods (including yogurt) and be very careful with probiotics while you stabilize your system. There are specific strains of probiotics that can be very helpful but you must do your research and consult with your doctor to ensure you aren't doing more harm than good. Just like with fermented foods, some (many) probiotics feed the exact strains of bacteria that produce histamine. As with everything else, things that are helpful for a healthy system can cause problems when your system is out of balance.

3. GETTING STARTED

This book doesn't follow all the rules for a low histamine diet because the first recommendation is almost always to eat a lot of uncooked fruits and vegetables, which is exactly counter to following an OAS diet. This is an attempt to balance the needs of the two diets and create something that isn't completely depressing that also provides moderate nutrition, while following the main guidelines. It generally follows more closely to OAS guidelines for the simple reason that they are simpler: no uncooked fruits and vegetables and be wary of spices. Histamine in food is also a newer area of study with more unknowns and variables. For a low histamine diet, there are lots of different "low histamine lists". Why? First and foremost, each person reacts slightly differently. Second, the older food is, the more histamine it is likely to contain because proteins are continually breaking down into histamines, etc. Food that is fine fresh may be on all the "no" lists if it's hard to find fresh enough (like fish). Third, it's not an area that has been studied in great depth or for a long time.

Recommendations in this book are based on a combination of specific information and consensus among the lists (where it exists), with a touch of reality. What I mean by that last is keeping in mind what is affordable, easy to find, and helps keep at least some variety in food groups, taste, and texture. Keeping all "leavening" out of a diet is tough (to say the least), but reducing it is doable, for example. The "SIGHI list" in Appendix 2 is the most specific and detailed histamine list I have found. Those 19 pages include less common foods like bak choi and venison. More importantly, it breaks out whether they are histamine liberating, high histamine, a blocker, decay quickly (releasing histamines) or contain other amines. It's a TON of information but it's surprisingly simple to use.

One limitation I think it's important to note is that most low-histamine lists focus on widely-available Western foods. There are sometimes great options from other cuisines, if you search for them. For example, wine and beer are discussed, but sake isn't. Sake is lower histamine than either of those and, unlike vodka, isn't made from an ingredient (potato) that can cause problems.

Some lists say not to eat poultry, meat, or really any kind of animal protein. That doesn't seem healthy or desirable for a month or longer. Poultry (chicken and turkey) and lamb have the least negative comments and are readily available (unlike venison, for example), so they are the main meats used in this book. Every effort was made to call out non-compliant ingredients in the recipe introduction but, as already noted, there isn't complete agreement on the lists. Because of this approach, there may still be some things that you react to and there are some recipes you may need to wait to eat, since this is intended as a longer-term resource. It is important to keep track of what you eat and any reactions you have.

There is a lot to take in so here are the first steps.

Go Basic, Go Simple

So, how to start? If you can't read and pronounce the full ingredient list, don't eat it, and that includes restaurant foods. That means you probably won't be eating out for a few weeks while you are on a strict version of this diet. You can find some basics you can eat as sold in the grocery store but not a lot. If Mother Nature wouldn't recognize the ingredients, don't eat it. **Avoid spices and herbs, initially, especially generic "spices" or "flavorings" that don't list exactly what they are. Continue avoiding foods with generic "spices" or "flavorings" indefinitely, to be safe.** If there are two or three spices you use all the time and are 100% confident you can use, go ahead and continue using them but try to eliminate them at least for a couple weeks just to be sure they aren't a hidden problem. Two weeks of spice-free food is doable.

Avoid sweets and things doctors already tell us all to avoid, such as caffeine. Avoid canned and prepacked goods. Artificial flavorings, colorings, and preservatives can trigger histamine production, which is exactly what you need to avoid. Simple foods like grilled cheese or a simple baked chicken are your best choices. Once I was past the initial elimination phase, I added canned food back into my diet because some days, we all need fast and easy. Plus, the truth is that a fair amount of canned veggies were already cooked pretty thoroughly. They don't taste as good, but it's a whole lot faster and easier than using fresh.

We all know the bad stuff that we aren't supposed to eat: anything we can't pronounce, processed sugar, white flour, white rice, caffeine, etc. I know that's repetitive, but this is the time you actually have to eliminate those things from your diet, for real, at least for a little while. That actually gets you a long way toward a healthier, low-histamine diet. Make sure all fruits and veggies are well-cooked for OAS issues. Chapter 4 goes into more detail but those basics will get you started and keep you generally going in the right direction as your body starts healing.

Accept that you will have to cook most of your food from scratch and you will need to read the ingredient list on _every-_ **_thing_**. I reacted when I ate half a slice of rye bread without reading the ingredients. It had garlic and onion powder, as do most packaged broth and stock packages. I'm allergic to both.

Oral Allergy Syndrome

For most fruits and vegetables (not celery), cooking damages or destroys the problematic proteins. In most cases, those with OAS can eat these foods if they are thoroughly cooked. For some foods, these proteins are concentrated in the skin. Peeling them before eating reduces reactions enough that some people may be able to eat them uncooked. **This isn't true for spices, nuts, and celery, so avoid**

these even when cooked. Also, dried herbs are less problematic than fresh.

Pureed foods are thoroughly cooked, then blended. *Deceptively Delicious* by Jessica Seinfeld does a great job describing how to puree a wide variety of foods and provides recipes that use pureed fruits and vegetables in unexpected ways. Celebrity wife or not, she's a busy mom and I recommend her books. None of her recipes are included here for the simple reason they don't need modified to be compliant and every recipe in this book was modified or from my personal recipes box.

Leftovers

If you have leftovers, **it's important to keep them cold and eat them quickly to prevent problems**. Freezing slows or stops most of these processes so food stays good longer than it does in the refrigerator. Thermal bags and coolers are your friends. If you have a long drive home from the grocery store, keep a cooler in your vehicle and store meat, dairy, and other cold items in it for the drive home on hot days. Oxygen leads food to break down more quickly. That's why vacuum-sealed food stays fresher, longer. **Better quality food storage containers**, with better quality seals, keep food fresher, longer. If leftovers have been in the fridge for a few days or sat in a hot summer car for an hour, they are no longer compliant with a low histamine diet. The proteins have almost certainly broken down and freed too much histamine to remain a safe choice. Even if you would normally consider them safe, they aren't right now, for you.

If you carry a lunch to work, which is likely given how hard it is to find low histamine/OAS food in cafeterias, use a good thermal lunch bag for your commute. Also, when you have a small amount of something left over, it may make a good sushi roll or two or a stir fry, which makes a great lunch. Sushi rolls are surprisingly simple to make and only use small amounts of "stuffing" per roll.

Keeping Track

It's boring and a bit of a pain, but it's important to keep a food diary. **Log everything you eat and any symptoms you have, every day, so you can track what foods cause symptoms.** Keep track of your medications, as well.

There's no nice way to say it, but you need to keep track of your bowel movements, too. Radical or even (relatively) minor dietary changes can lead to constipation or diarrhea. Letting those go unchecked can have bad consequences for your body. Of course, they may also help you be more regular, and it's good to know that too. Or, as a friend's daughter says, "If you don't poop, you die." So, pay attention, and remember to eat fiber. Oats can be your friend.

As you go through this, apps are your friends too. "Cara" is a food tracking app that also allows you to track symptoms/reactions. In the "Intolerances" app, you select filters for food intolerances including low histamine, FODMAPS, gluten, and more. Foods are colored from green (safe) to red (avoid), including serving size, histamine amounts, and if they are a histamine liberator. Some foods include specific explanations of why they are/aren't safe. It's hard to describe just how much easier apps can make navigating these challenges, especially in the beginning.

Hard Nos

This is a lot of information and it can be hard to keep straight. Here is a list of **the most problematic foods**, the ones that you should work hardest to eliminate entirely, particularly in the elimination phase:

- Raw fruits, vegetables, and berries (OAS)
- Spices (yes, all of them – except salt)
- Ketchup and tomato products
- Most condiments, including soy sauce
- Vinegar
- Pickles and pickled anything
- Fermented food, including sauerkraut and yogurt

- Fish and shellfish
- Smoked meats, including ham and sausage
- Beef and all jerky
- Soured food, including sour cream and sourdough bread
- Aged food, including most cheese
- Drinks other than water, plain milk, and decaf coffee
- Canned food (for histamine, can be better for OAS)
- Alcohol, especially red wine

I know: Gee, is that all? No, that's not all but those are the biggest culprits. That's why I wrote this. While they are hard no's on a low histamine elimination diet, that doesn't mean you won't ever be able to eat them again. When your body is struggling with allergens and you have to pull back to a stricter low histamine diet for a bit, remove these first. They are also ones you should work hardest to limit, but limit isn't the same as avoid entirely, unless they are problematic *for you*.

The recipes in this book aren't the most exciting meals in the world, lacking spices and fresh fruit/vegetables, but there is a lot of variety. These are just a starting point. As you get used to this, you can add food you enjoy back into your diet. I certainly didn't figure out all of these in the first day, or even the first month, I was on this diet. I never would have guessed cumin was a problem if I hadn't done this elimination diet, and if I hadn't been very careful and purposeful when I added new ingredients to my meals.

My friends and family asked when I would know I was done with this cookbook. The answer was "when I can regularly look through and find something I want to eat without feeling deprived." When I first thought I was almost done, I realized I needed sauces so I went back and added an entire chapter of sauces.

Grocery Items You Can (Probably) Eat

When you need something quick, like on the first day or two of this diet, while traveling, or if you get sick, these items are easy to grab from the grocery store. **Remember to read the entire ingredi-**

ent list to be sure there aren't problematic additives or trace ingredients.

Applesauce

Plain applesauce, without added cinnamon or other flavorings.

Cheese and Crackers

    Young cheese, nothing aged
    Grated Parmesan, not aged
    Cream Cheese
    Crackers

If you eat too much cheese, it can cause constipation, so keep track of your "ins and outs" along with your food diary. Aged cheese is a problem, so stick with young cheeses including mild cheddar (*not* sharp) and Gouda (not aged). Parmesan cheese in a can (already grated) is generally young cheese, so it's OK. Parmesan sold in blocks is far more likely to be aged, and aged cheese should be avoided.

Many kinds of crackers, including saltines and water crackers, are compliant but read the ingredients list to be sure, and there is a short chapter with cracker recipes.

Cottage Cheese with Fruit

    2 c. cottage cheese
    1 tsp. jam/preserves or berry compote (recipe on page 70)

Mix together. Eat. It is not exciting but it is a change from plain cottage cheese.

Granola

This can be a great snack but read the ingredient list carefully. Try to find one with no nuts and be careful to avoid chocolate and additives.

Grits

A Southern staple, this simple dish goes well with chicken and simply adding cheese gives it a new dimension. It is often sold in ready-to-make containers similar to oatmeal.

Ice Cream

Look for one with simple ingredients that you can pronounce. Vanilla is the safest choice since it has the fewest ingredients. As with everything else, chocolate is a potential histamine issue.

Oatmeal

This is one of the easiest foods to find and to carry with you when you travel. It's always good to have an emergency meal on hand when you have significant food allergy issues.

> ½ c. oatmeal
>
> 1 c. water

Add-ins:

> 1 tsp. honey (local, raw)
> Jam/preserves
> Maple syrup
> Berry compote (recipe on page 70)
> Cranberry sauce (recipe on page 74)

Mix the oatmeal and water and microwave for 90 seconds. Mix the honey or other add-ins into the oatmeal. The honey will melt, so it's okay if it solidified.

Plain old Quaker Oats™ works just fine. I always wondered about the difference between steel cut, regular, and quick cooking. Steel cut is the least processed and quick cooking is the most processed. Regular (rolled) oats are steamed to make them soft and then rolled flat. Quick cooking are cooked, dried, and then flattened thinner than rolled oats, which also results in them breaking up into smaller pieces. Nutritionally, they are all about the same.

Pasta

Most pasta is not much more than wheat or another grain. You can cook it and add olive oil and some simple chunks of chicken, roasted vegetables, or whatever else suits.

Tortellini and Stuffed Pasta

Read the ingredient list but cheese-filled tortellini and other stuffed pasta (e.g., ravioli, pierogis) are worth trying. Avoid complex or "exotic" stuffing, including squash and other vegetables, and read the ingredients carefully. Cook, coat with olive oil, and eat.

Wraps

Tortillas

Turkey or chicken

Gouda or cream cheese

Fill center of tortilla with sandwich ingredients. Fold the edges over to completely cover the filling.

4. General Guidelines

Now that you understand the basics, here are some guidelines and specifics on categories of food. Personally, I ended up eating small amounts of some of these ingredients even on the elimination diet because I couldn't eliminate every single thing that might be a problem, but they were <u>very</u> small amounts compared to my normal diet, and I cut out soda and caffeine entirely during the elimination phase. For example, when I was craving something–anything!–sweet, I had about a quarter cup of rice pudding instead of several cookies or a soda. It still had sugar, but a much smaller amount.

The hard and ironic part of this whole thing is that many otherwise healthy foods can create problems for people on OAS and low histamine diets. That's another reason keeping a food diary is so important.

Bread, Yeast, and Leavening

There is a lot of conflicting information about bread, mostly because of yeast. Some places say nothing with any kind of yeast but other places list different kinds of bread as acceptable. From what I have read, the problem isn't yeast per se but contamination that can occur, sometimes. Yeast <u>extract</u>, on the other hand, is a common high histamine additive to spicy foods. The bottom line is that bread may cause problems so pay attention but you probably don't need to eliminate it entirely.

Here's a simple test: **If bread smells yeasty, try another kind.** Sourdough, in particular, is called out as a poor choice for a low histamine diet, but for other reasons. **Anything that has been "soured", including sour cream and sourdough, can be a histamine problem.** Read the ingredients carefully, even for bread. Rye bread is specifically listed as good but as I ate a piece of rye toast, I started having an allergic reaction. It never occurred to me that garlic would be in rye bread, but it was. **Read the ingredient list for everything** to be sure there aren't any additives or unexpected ingredients that will impact you, no matter what kind you choose or how often you have eaten it before.

Cooking

The way food is cooked impacts histamine levels. Smoking definitely leads to higher histamine levels, which is why smoked foods such as ham are on the no lists. An interesting Korean study of frying, grilling, and boiling (Appendix 1) found that grilling and frying can both increase histamine levels but boiling doesn't. Cooking food at high temperatures (such as grilling) increases histamine levels more than cooking at lower temperatures (such as boiling or using a sous vide). Another cooking method worth trying is steaming food, fruits and veggies in particular. This doesn't work for everyone but at least it may add some variety. While the preferred cooking methods in Korea vary from common methods in the US, that study demonstrates that cooking methods impact food histamine levels. Food that is problematic cooked one way may be fine cooked another way.

I'm not a gourmet cook by any stretch of the imagination but even I can cook a variety of different ways including baking, sautéing, roasting, frying, grilling, and boiling–and even using a sous vide! It's daunting when you first look at it but the truth is that most people have done all of those except using a sous vide, and that's really just a fancy, gadgety way to boil things. You have to follow directions, not learn fancy techniques. Each of those techniques has the potential to give you new meals, textures, and tastes to enjoy. What's not to enjoy about that?

Drinks

Water is compliant. Also, decaffeinated coffee, plain (not flavored) sparkling water, and club soda. So, basically a few variations on water, but don't infuse it with berries, cucumbers, etc. since those can trigger OAS. **Milk is your other compliant option** (no added flavor).

No caffeine, so no sodas or caffeinated coffee.

No tea, including herbal tea, although plain green tea may be acceptable in small amounts. In addition to being on many low histamine no lists, herbal tea is just too much risk of a cross-reaction with OAS unless you are extraordinarily careful. Chamomile is on the OAS list, for example, but many herbal teas contain extracts, leaves, etc. from a wide variety of fruits. In addition, some have caffeine, which is on the no list. It's safer and easier to just skip it for a few weeks, or remove it from your diet entirely.

Juice should be avoided for OAS, unless the fruit/veggie has no risk of cross-reacting or is cooked first (Roasted Orange Juice, page 90), but some non-citrus juices are compliant with low histamine diets. Citrus and strawberries are on both "no" lists, making fruity mixed drinks with alcohol like margaritas and daiquiris huge no-nos.

No alcohol. Alcohol in virtually all forms is a histamine liberator and should be avoided. (Vodka, gin, white rum are the only identified exceptions but if you can't eat potatoes, don't drink vodka.) Beer and wine are fermented, another no. In addition to alcohol and fermentation, red wine has high histamine levels, is a histamine liberator, and inhibits DAO from working. **Red wine is a <u>huge</u> no.** It has high histamine levels (60 to 3,800 micrograms of histamine per glass). If you have a special event and want to enjoy an adult beverage, white wine (3-120 micrograms of histamine per glass) is a far safer choice. Rosé (15-60 micrograms) is also a much lower histamine choice. (White wines have lower histamine levels but higher levels of sulfites, so they aren't necessarily easier on your body.)

I recently stumbled across something called "The Wine Wand" by PureWine. It is a disposable filter used to remove sulfites and histamines from wine. I haven't tried them yet but the reviews are great and if you enjoy wine, it's worth at least looking at their information. Sake is another potential option. It is said to be low in histamine but I haven't found any specific information to compare it directly to wine.

Most smoothies are not compliant because yogurt, most fresh fruit, and most fresh vegetables are not compliant. It is possible to make compliant smoothies (this book includes one) but, like most things, you probably won't find them in the average store.

Fermentation, Including Pickling

A gigantic no-no, fermentation is one reason alcohol (especially red wine and beer) is off the list with a low-histamine diet. **Fermented dairy products include yogurt, kefir, buttermilk, sour cream, and aged cheese need to be avoided.** Some lists remove all cheese, including cream cheese and cottage cheese, but most lists don't go that far. Most allow cream cheese, cottage cheese, and young, soft cheese. Again, it depends on your body.

Pickling (pickles, pickled eggs, Kimchee, sauerkraut, and other foods prepared with vinegar) is also problematic for anyone with histamine intolerance. **Fermented soy products (miso, soy sauce, tempeh) are yet another problem.** Going back to the science explanation in Chapter 2, pickling cause proteins to break down and release amines, particularly histamine.

Eating too much fermented food can create gut issues by causing histamine-producing gut bacteria to overgrow.

Fruits and Veggies

It feels wrong, but you need to **avoid both fresh and dehydrated fruit if you have OAS.** The high temperatures in cooking damages or destroys the allergens in most fruit but dehydrating doesn't get them hot enough, making dehydrated fruit also something to generally avoid. Applesauce and banana bread are both examples of fruits that are baked enough to be safe on an OAS diet.

Citrus fruits, in particular, are suspected histamine liberators, as well as being potential OAS cross-reactors. There may be some you can safely eat but you need to research that for yourself and talk to your doctor. Initially, the easiest and safest route is to avoid problematic ones and thoroughly cook any you do eat.

Berries are a mixed bag. Strawberries are a hard no (OAS and histamine issues) and raspberries are also a no, but blueberries and blackberries are generally compliant.

The primary vegetables to avoid on a low histamine diet are spinach, celery, eggplant, cabbage, and tomatoes. Tomato is probably the most important, and difficult, vegetable to avoid. OAS has more restrictions but they are on fresh vegetables, not cooked ones. Celery is an exception and should be avoided entirely if it's a potential OAS issue for you (tree pollen allergies) as the allergens do not seem to be sufficiently damaged by cooking. **As with fruits, make sure veggies are extremely well cooked.**

Meat, Seafood, and Poultry

Protein triggers the gut to release DAO (which is good) but the restrictions on this diet can lead to eating less protein. Make the effort to eat protein regularly. Appendix 1 includes a link to easy protein swaps that is worth reading. Interestingly, marinades and rubs can help prevent amines from forming during cooking and they are a great way to add flavor without a lot of problematic ingredients.

Most fish and all shellfish should be avoided, unless they are freshly caught. If you really must have fish, the worst ones for histamine are tuna, mackerel, Mahi Mahi, anchovy, herring, bluefish, amberjack and marlin, so at least avoid those.

Micro-organisms in fish guts start breaking down proteins as soon as fish die, resulting in ever-increasing levels of histamines until they are gutted. If you gut and cook a fish within a half hour of catching, enjoy! That pretty much means you are there when it's caught, or you are at restaurant and choose a live one from a tank. If it's commercially caught and happens to be the last one gutted and frozen, you're almost certainly subjecting your body to much higher histamine levels. Since shellfish are never gutted, they continue to break down proteins and produce histamines until they are cooked. That's why shellfish are such a hard no on this diet.

Since seafood (cooked or raw) and fresh vegetables should be avoided, sushi is problematic but not impossible. In short: **you are unlikely to be able to buy it can make your own sushi** using fully cooked ingredients, or fresh-caught fish.

Avoid smoked meats including ham, sausage, bacon, deli meat, and jerky. Smoking is problematic.

Avoid skin, including chicken skin. Remove the skin before you even cook your food because poultry cooked with the skin on has higher amine levels even after the skin is removed. (The skin is normally removed from beef and turned into leather long before it reaches the supermarket.)

Beef is also on the "no" list, especially ground beef. I'm not entirely sure why but my allergist was firm on this. I assume it's related to the way beef is processed. Hamburger (ground beef) is an even bigger no because the greater exposed surface area means the proteins in it break down faster and histamines increase more rapidly.

Lamb is your friend.

Poultry (chicken and turkey) is also your friend, but avoid ground versions unless you use them immediately, for the same reasons as ground beef. It's worth taking a shot and asking if the butcher can grind your meat while you wait. If you remain on a generally low-histamine diet, you might want to simply buy a meat grinder for your own home use. An attachment for a Kitchenaid® mixer is only $40 and standalone models (electric and hand operated) are affordable as well.

Miscellaneous

Chocolate isn't compliant, except for white chocolate. Generally, to be considered "chocolate", it has to contain chocolate liquor (which is not alcohol at all), cocoa butter, and cocoa solids. Of the three, "white chocolate" only contains cocoa butter, and cocoa butter doesn't cause histamine issues. As a result, many people can tolerate it without the problems "real" chocolate can cause, but it's still important to check the ingredient list and note any symptoms you have. Some brands contain problematic ingredients such as soy or sunflower lecithin.

Most nuts are not compliant on a low-histamine diet and peanuts can be problematic for OAS, so **eliminate nuts, especially walnuts**, during the elimination phase. Many seeds, such as sunflower seeds, can also cause histamine problems. Chia seeds are OK.

Eggs are definitely on both approved lists, although uncooked egg whites are considered a histamine liberator. My first thought was really, who eats uncooked eggs, unless they are in cookie dough? When I looked into it a little more, eggnog (and cookie dough) went onto the no list, so there are some things with uncooked egg whites. Meringue and cream pies (topped with meringue) are probably best avoided, too.

Pre-shredded cheese can contain corn starch or other additives to prevent clumping. Cheddar cheese is naturally white but "annatto" is often added to make it the orange color most of us know. Annatto is produced from an evergreen tree/shrub, so it is possible to have a reaction to orange, but not white, cheddar. (There is a link in Appendix 1 for more information on annatto.) Annatto is a surprisingly common additive, so be sure to note it in your food diary.

Seaweed

Considering how popular sushi is, it took a ridiculous amount of time to find histamine information on it. I found that it depends on the kind of seaweed. Based on what I can read, the best kinds are wakame, nori, kombu, and hijiki, although there is conflicting information. (The SIGHI List shows nori as a histamine liberator that should be avoided.) Luckily, those seem to be the most common kinds in the US with nori being a standard choice for sushi. So, pick up some seaweed, but read the ingredients. Many have added seasoning. If it isn't in English, look for a brand that is.

Spices

Basically, your diet will be incredibly bland for at least a few weeks, just to be safe, and you will need to add spices back gradually, just like other foods. **"With spices" should be taken as a giant red flag and strictly avoided since you have no idea what they are.** While many spices are probably fine, given how many are out there, histamine in foods is a particularly recent area of study so there are a lot of unknowns and, unlike fruits and vegetables, heat doesn't break down the problematic proteins in spices. During the elimination phase, spices aren't worth the risk. **The safest spices for this diet are ginger, turmeric, nigella, and garlic. The worst spices are anise and paprika, which are on both lists.**

A surprisingly large number of spices are related to trees and other plants, making them a no-go for OAS. For OAS, **specific spices to avoid include anise, basil, caraway, coriander, cumin, dill, fennel, marjoram, mustard, oregano, parsley, paprika, pepper, tarragon, and thyme.** Although pepper is a potential problem, I left it in because it is the one spice that's always available. Just be aware and you may want to eliminate it initially.

Low-histamine restricted spices include cinnamon, chili powder, cloves, anise, nutmeg, curry, and paprika. Low-histamine friendly spices include ginger, turmeric, coriander, thyme, **nigella, and garlic.** (Coriander and thyme have OAS issues.)

Plain old salt (in moderation) is okay but it really should be a low- or non-processed sea salt. Most table salt has been processed to add iodine and remove impurities, which also removes trace elements and minerals. Your body will really need those trace elements even more while you are on this diet. Two good choices are pink Himalayan Sea Salt and gray Celtic Sea Salt. Appendix 1 (Additional Resources) has a link with more detailed information on specific kinds of salt. Normally it might not seem worth the effort to learn about different kinds of salt, but if your spice intake remains limited for long, it's worth it. It's also worth learning how to make your own flavored salt. If you can't find healthier kinds of salt anywhere local, you can definitely order them online.

Vinegar

Vinegar is another hard no for low-histamine diets, which is another reason pickled things are not compliant. White vinegar is clearly a no but I found conflicting verdicts on apple cider vinegar. Based on what I have read, **organic apple cider vinegar that still contains the mother may be tolerable**, but it's not great. Regular apple cider vinegar is probably slightly better than white vinegar but should still be avoided. It's really pretty simple to tell which apple cider vinegar contains the mother: the labels clearly state it contains the mother, plus it tends to be cloudy at the bottom, like high pulp orange juice when the pulp has settled.

Sadly, vinegar is a key component in many condiments, including ketchup and mustard, so **it's best to steer clear of condiments.** Since ketchup is tomato-based, this double-whammy makes traditional ketchup a hard no on a low-histamine diet.

As your health improves and you start adding ingredients back, start with apple cider with the mother, then regular apple cider if needed, and avoid regular white vinegar as much and long as possible.

5. Low Histamine Holidays

Human nature seems to naturally tie food traditions to major holidays, especially if the whole tribe gathers together. Eating a low histamine/OAS diet is challenging enough for an individual, couple, or family, but figuring out something the extended family will eat can be a nightmare, especially if other people have allergies to accommodate. It's important to remember that everyone doesn't have to be able to eat every dish, including family members who live with you. They need enough food to eat a satisfying meal, including dessert, and to not feel left out. A good compromise is making food the person with restrictions can eat, putting other ingredients in separate bowls with separate utensils. Others can mix those in. For example, my family routinely adds spices to the spice-free meals I make.

Convincing your loving family (parents) that many "healthy" foods are not healthy for you can be a major challenge. Everyone has heard the "fact" that cooking fruits and veggies destroys what makes them so healthy, which can make it difficult to believe that you really can't eat them raw. Don't feel guilty for asking for something different or bringing food for yourself. If you can't eat it, you can't eat it. And never, ever feel guilty for asking to look at packaging to ensure it's safe for you. You know trace ingredients can be a real problem for allergies. Other people's conviction that you can eat something doesn't change how your body reacts. Don't risk a reaction!

It's also important to remember that histamine levels can build over time. If you eat a low-histamine diet on a day-to-day basis, "cheating" a bit on holidays shouldn't be a big problem, especially if most of your meal is still compliant. Hopefully these suggestions will help you create holiday celebrations everyone can enjoy. Enjoy yourself a little!

Alcohol

There are a lot of special events and holidays when adults would like to be able to enjoy an adult beverage, but histamine issues can make that hard. Beer and wine are both problematic because they are fermented, and because alcohol is generally a histamine liberator. Vodka is made from potatoes, so it can be a problem for people who react to nightshades.

Mixed Drinks

If you like mixed drinks, vodka, gin, and white rum are compliant, but be careful of what they are mixed with. And again, beware vodka if you can't eat potatoes.

Wine

White and rosé wine can both have comparatively reasonable histamine levels, but higher levels of potentially problematic sulfites. Sparkling wine (champagne) isn't great but some may be tolerable. Beer is better than champagne but higher histamine than white or rosé. Red wine is another story and far more likely to lead to problematic reactions. For special days in particular, the WineWand can make a huge difference in how wine impacts you by reducing the sulfites and histamine level.

Sake

The generic Japanese word for what Americans call sake (the Japanese word for alcohol) means "wine of Japan" but sake also shares some similarity with beer. While it is definitely a different beverage, good sake can be both enjoyed and stored similarly to wine. Sake is low histamine and far less acidic than wine. Pasteurization allows it to be preservative-free (no sulfites). Unlike wine, sake is usually best within one or two years of bottling and is better fresher.

The first sake brands imported were low quality and were served hot to help mask that. Today, that is no longer necessary, so you can enjoy sake chilled, room temperature, or hot, depending on the sake. "Junmai" sake only has the fewest ingredients, so it's a good place to start, if you want to try sake. If you want to learn more about sake, there are links in Appendix 2.

Birthdays

The biggest issue with birthdays is cakes. They can be spiced or include fruit filling or toppings. Sadly, the berry tarts I love are out for now. Ice cream cake can be a good alternative, as long as dairy isn't a problem, since spices and uncooked fruits and veggies are almost never in ice cream cakes. The same is true for cheesecake and the egg-heavy thousand layer cake. Berry compote over cake can make something plain into a tasty treat.

Valentine's Day

For adults, this is a holiday built on chocolate and fancy restaurant meals. For kids, it's all about the chocolate. Either way, it can be a challenge. Boxes of chocolates rarely state what is in each chocolate, and we all know how challenging it is to figure out what any individual candy is. On top of that, cross-contamination is a real issue. Boxes of chocolate, unfortunately, are probably best avoided.

This might be the perfect day for a Thousand Layer cake. Tailor the flavored layer to whatever you and your beloved both enjoy and can eat. If you add berry compote with raspberry or cherry to a Thousand Layer Cake with chocolate layers instead of spice, then you even have the signature red of Valentine's Day.

Valentine's might also be a good time to take a class in making chocolates. If actual chocolate is a problem but white chocolate is tolerated, then you can make a box of white chocolates, which is beyond rare in stores. If chocolate is tolerated, then you can just make sure there aren't any other problematic ingredients in the box. Then you can give your love their own homemade box of chocolates.

Easter

Read the ingredients and be careful with candy and chocolate.

The big non-candy Easter challenge is ham. Ham is almost always smoked and therefore not low histamine. The simple solution is to eat lamb instead of ham. One lamb recipe is included in Chapter 16 but it is easy to find great lamb recipes online and in cookbooks.

Hard boiled eggs, decorated and hidden for the egg hunt, are a beloved tradition. If the egg hunt is short and the day cool, the eggs are probably still safe to eat if they are stored in the fridge before and after, cleaned well, and not broken. But not if you have histamine issues. Don't take chances. Toss the eggs after the egg hunt.

Picnics (Labor Day, Fourth of July, Memorial Day)

Hot dogs, bratwurst, and hamburgers. Fresh fruit and berries. Salad. Vine ripened tomatoes. All summer classics, none of them compliant. Naturally, grilling, in general, also increases histamine levels. So what's the answer? For a main course, make a burger with ground chicken or turkey instead of ground beef (such as the Cheesy Black Bean Burgers, page 146) or have chicken breasts, another summer classic. You could also make a veggie burger, provided you fully cook it. Better yet, find some casseroles you enjoy and bring those to picnics.

Side dishes are a bit harder and require some advance prep to ensure fruits and veggies are fully and completely cooked. Deviled eggs (page 100) are an example of a compliant version of a classic appetizer, readily available online. A simple sliced mini baguette of bread and a good olive oil to dip it in is another simple, healthy side many can appreciate, especially if the bread is fresh.

Thanksgiving and Christmas

Since turkey is compliant, the main dish is pretty simple, especially if you roast it. Like ham, smoked turkey isn't a compliant option because smoked foods are not low histamine. Sticking to roast turkey is the easiest solution. Some classics, such as cranberry sauce, aren't compliant (cranberries are generally on no lists, although others list them as low-histamine) but this book includes best versions. These versions are less likely to cause issues because they have been simplified, but use moderation.

Stuffing is another potential landmine because it has so many ingredients, including celery, which you should skip. The good news is you can modify your favorite recipe by omitting ingredients and substituting others, such as by using matzo in stuffing. You just have to cook it yourself.

In addition, there are some great side dish recipes in Chapter 14 such as green beans, corn pudding, mashed maple squash, and honey ginger carrots. Corn on the cob doesn't really require a recipe but it's another great addition to holiday meals. Chapter 18 includes classic holiday desserts such as gingerbread and sugar cookies. Believe me, I know how daunting this can be, but it *is* doable to create an appetizing low-histamine holiday feast, especially when you add in other allergies. My family did it!

New Year's Eve and Parties

Holidays have different food challenges based on where you live. In some areas, sauerkraut is a New Years' staple but it is definitely not compliant. Party appetizers and finger foods are challenges everywhere. Salami and other common cracker (deli) meats should be avoided as should veggie trays (OAS), but cheese and crackers are generally safe. (Skip cheese with herbs, peppers, or anything else in it, including cheeseballs, just to be safe.) There are probably chips and even dips you can safely eat but you need to figure that out for yourself, in advance, or skip them. At a party is not the time to experiment.

For most people, the main New Year's Eve challenges are alcohol and fruit juice (sparkling cider, for example) being on the list of foods to avoid. If you're in the northern hemisphere and it's the middle of the winter, your OAS symptoms may be under control enough to allow sparkling cider. If you're in the southern hemisphere or near the equator, it could be more challenging. If you really want to toast in the New Year, choose your beverage thoughtfully.

There is more detail on alcoholic beverages earlier in this chapter, but, in short, you should be able to comfortably ring in the New Year with an adult beverage, if you keep the indulgence moderate.

6. Next Steps

Hopefully you remember that you should only do this under a doctor's care and guidance, and most people shouldn't be on a strict version of this for more than a few weeks, especially without medical guidance, but there's nothing wrong with including these recipes as part of your family's regular diet. They are healthy and tasty, if sometimes a bit bland, but adding herbs and spices is simple. As you move forward with re-introducing foods, it's very important to continue a food diary to see what foods or food combinations cause you problems and to add new foods slowly. Review your food diary regularly to look for patterns and foods that cause or relieve problems.

With OAS, you may be able to add foods back in based on the season and when you are exposed to different pollens, then remove them again when your exposure is high. Unfortunately, dietary changes related to histamine intolerance are probably more long-term. Even then, you should still be able to add <u>some</u> (not necessarily all) foods back as your overall histamine level decreases. This is when you should start a trial-and-error process to figure out what your body tolerates well and what it doesn't, which is where a food diary really matters, and where the lists of tolerated foods, herbs, and spices in the back will come in handy.

Explore new foods! It's no secret that allergies get worse with repeated exposure, which means your "old favorites" are more likely to cause problems because you've had a lot of exposure. Experiment! Try new fruits and veggies! I find lots of different options at Asian,

Indian, and Latino markets. The ones near me also typically have as a large selection of fresh herbs, fruits, and vegetables, including ones that don't sell rapidly in grocers catering to Western tastes, and ingredients like sushi rice that may not be readily available, fresh, or inexpensive in other markets.

Before you see your doctor for follow-up appointments, think about what foods you missed the most and want to try adding back in. You might be surprised when you stop to think about it. I missed cinnamon even more than sweets or chocolate, although it only beat chocolate by a hair. More importantly, if I can eat cinnamon, I can eat a lot of foods that include cinnamon, especially breakfast foods. While I also miss pickled foods, primarily pickled eggs, it isn't been worth the risk to add them back. If this diet helps you, there is a good chance you and your doctor will keep you on some version of it indefinitely. If so, it's even more important to learn how to modify foods you love so you can continue to eat them and to learn what you really must avoid, to make eating out easier. The Appendixes are there to help you integrate low histamine elements into your diet in a safe and maintainable way.

Once you know your personal triggers, it's time to suck it up and clean out the pantry, the fridge, and the spice rack, reading all the ingredient lists (including spice mixes) to avoid potential problems. I started small with the spice rack, then the fridge, the pantry, and the freezer. I gave food to family, friends, and the local food pantry. (The food pantry wouldn't take half a loaf of bread; Mom was happy to.) Now you know you can pull out food from your own pantry and be safe. If you don't live alone, you may keep some things you can't eat, but it should be easier to keep track after your Great Cleanout.

Once you know what you can and can't eat, going to restaurants and eating pre-packaged convenience foods may be doable for you again, or not. With a garlic allergy, the answer is pretty well "not." As a result, I bought a few additional home appliances to make it easier to cook tastier meals for myself. We already have a good slow cooker but recently added a high-quality meat grinder and sous vide. I refuse to feel guilty for spending money on these because my restaurant options are so limited.

Create a list of very low-histamine foods/meals that work for you. You can pull back and eat those "safe meals" as needed for a meal or a few days, allowing your body to calm down. When you hit a rough patch with your symptoms, or if other allergies temporarily flare out of control, go back to these safe meals. It can also be helpful eating out or at someone else's house. For example, I know I can eat bread with (un-infused) olive oil, which is easy to find at restaurants or friend's homes.

Most of these recipes are quite basic. That makes it easy to mix-and-match them, so please try it! The chicken breast, roasted white sauce, and manicotti stuffed with goat cheese are all tasty. Absolutely nothing is stopping you from combining them into a new meal, as just one example.

Finally, when you eat out, you may feel like Sally in *When Harry Met Sally*, especially at first. (Google "sally order when harry met sally" if you don't know the scene.) That's okay. You aren't ordering an item without half the ingredients and the sauce to be picky. You are doing it because you don't have a choice, and that's just how it is. Lots of people have allergy issues so there is a lot more understanding today than there would have been thirty years ago.

7. SEASONING

I t's tough to cook every single meal and snack from scratch. Most of us just don't have that much time, but pre-made meals (and seasonings) can be tough if you have allergies. This section has some seasonings you can make ahead in larger batches to speed up the process other nights, like shake and bake.

Spices let you add flavor with a relatively small amount of an ingredient. If there is a <u>slightly</u> problematic food you truly miss, this is one way you may be able to enjoy a little of that flavor. As with everything, add new ingredients slowly and keep a food diary noting any changes or reactions, then avoid those foods. Once you try a recipe or two, get creative and make your own, or search online for more recipes and substitutions. I just read that bee balm can be substituted for oregano, for example. (I haven't tried it.)

<u>With everything here, change the amounts of herbs and flavorings to suit your own taste and tolerance. Some may need to be removed entirely, and that's OK.</u>

Flavored salt can be added to foods at the very end, as a finishing flourish. Herbed salt can be used for a meat or vegetable rub, a marinade base, or in place of "regular" salt. Similarly, the herbed salts are good for adding a bit of extra flavor when you are cooking more than for putting on, say, a slice of toast or a baked potato.

Because my allergies to spices are so extensive, I could not try many of these recipes. For most of these, no ingredients are listed as "optional" because you should pick and choose what you can have.

Flavored Butter

It sounds odd at first, but it is a nice way to add some flavor.

Cinnamon Butter

Personally, I think the cinnamon butter is lovely on toast or croissants. It provides a hint of cinnamon flavor without actually eating a lot of cinnamon.

⅛ tsp. cinnamon

Melt butter. Stir in other ingredients. Store until needed.

Garlic Butter

¼ c. butter, cubed

1 garlic clove, minced

Melt butter. Stir in other ingredients. Store until needed.

Herbed Butter

¼ c. butter, cubed

⅛ tsp. dried rosemary, crushed

⅛ tsp. dried basil

⅛ tsp. dried marjoram

⅛ tsp. dried thyme

Melt butter. Stir in other ingredients. Store until you need to use it. You can use this with veggies or on bread.

Original Source: TasteofHome.com (Herb-Buttered Baby Carrots)

Lavender Butter

¼ c. butter, cubed

⅛ tsp. dried lavender, crushed

⅛ tsp. dried rosemary, crushed

Melt butter. Stir in other ingredients. Store until needed.

Flavored Salt

Basic Recipe

Combine ingredients in a clean coffee grinder or small food processor. (If you use a coffee grinder, make sure the primary coffee drinker knows and approves.) Use coarse salt, such as sea salt or kosher salt. Pulse until all ingredients are uniformly small. Store the herbed salt in a glass jar, such as an empty vitamin jar. Put a small amount of rice in the bottom if moisture is a concern.

With liquids such as vanilla or lemon juice, sprinkle the liquid over the salt before grinding to ensure even distribution, rather than pouring it all into one spot. Herbs should be dry but not brown. Dry salt with fresh herbs or moist ingredients like garlic or maple syrup by baking in the oven for 1-2 hours at 170-180°F. It may need to be ground a second time after cooling.

Garlic Salt

½ c. salt

2 cloves garlic

Garlic can be roasted or not. Crush cloves and chop with salt.

Herbed Salt

½ c. salt

10 sprigs of dried herbs such as rosemary or lemon balm

Destem and coarsely chop herbs.

Lavender Salt

½ c. salt

3 tsp. dried lavender

Maple Syrup Salt

½ c. salt

2 tsp. maple syrup

Mushroom Salt

½ c. salt

½ oz. dried shitake mushrooms

Rosemary and Lemon Salt

½ c. salt

3 tsp. dried lemon zest

3 tsp. dried rosemary

For fresh lemon zest, remove the outer zest with a microplane zester. Use only the outer part, not the bitter inner part. Dry on a towel. Destem and coarsely chop rosemary. Combine ingredients.

Original Source: MommyPotamus.com (Flavored Salt)

Burger Seasoning

4 Tbsp. pepper

2 tsp. salt

½ Tbsp. brown sugar

½ Tbsp. garlic powder

½ Tbsp. onion powder

Optional Ingredients (add as your diet allows):

2 Tbsp. paprika

1 tsp. cumin

Combine ingredients. Use about 1½ tsp. per pound of ground beef, then make burgers.

Original Source: CopyKat.com (Burger Seasoning Mix)

Italian Seasoning

3 Tbsp. dried basil

3 Tbsp. dried oregano

3 Tbsp. dried parsley

1 Tbsp. granulated garlic

1 tsp. granulated onion

1 tsp. dried rosemary

1 tsp. dried thyme

¼ tsp. black pepper

3 bay leaves

Combine ingredients. Pulse in a food processor until bay leaves are finely chopped.

Original Source: ItIsAKeeper.com (Italian Seasoning Mix)

Onion/Garlic/Tomato Powder

Tomatoes are definitely not compliant, but onion and garlic are. If you have a bumper crop of any of these, this is a great way to save some for later and have powder with zero additives.

Onions, garlic or tomatoes

Seed and slice before dehydrating. Dehydrate for several hours in the oven or a dehydrator, until dry and crispy. Once you have crispy slices, break them into small pieces and turn them into powder using your food processor or blender.

When I made this with my food processor, so much powder worked its way between the lid and the body of the container that it stuck. I dumped it upside down and shook all the powder out through the feeder opening, then rinsed it with water until it finally opened.

Parmesan Pizza Topping

½ c. grated parmesan cheese

1 tsp. basil

1 tsp. oregano

1 tsp. red pepper flakes

½ tsp. garlic powder

½ tsp. sea salt

Combine. Store. Sprinkle on pizza.

Original Source: AsTheBunnyHops.com (Parmesan Pizza Seasoning)

Poultry Seasoning

2 tsp. sage

1½ tsp. thyme

1 tsp. marjoram

¾ tsp. rosemary

½ tsp. nutmeg

½ tsp. black powder

Combine. Store. Rub on outside of chicken before roasting.

Original Source: LivingOnADime.com (Homemade Seasonings)

Pumpkin Spice Seasoning

4½ Tbsp. cinnamon

1 Tbsp. ginger

1 Tbsp. nutmeg

1 Tbsp. allspice

2 tsp. ground cloves

Optional Ingredients (add as your diet allows):

2 Tbsp. paprika

1 tsp. cumin

Combine ingredients.

Ranch Seasoning Mix

¾ c. dried parsley

3 Tbsp. dried dill

2 Tbsp. dried chives

¼ c. garlic powder

¼ c. onion powder

¼ c. dried onion flakes

2 Tbsp. kosher salt

2 Tbsp. ground black pepper

Pinch of cayenne pepper

Combine in a food processor and pulse for 1-2 minutes, until well mixed. You can store this in a refrigerator for up to 3 months.

Ranch Dressing

> 2 Tbsp. ranch seasoning mix
> ½ c. sour cream or yogurt
> 1 c. buttermilk
> 1 c. mayonnaise

To make ranch dressing, mix 2 Tbsp. of mix with ½ c. sour cream, 1 c. buttermilk, and 1 c. mayonnaise.

Original Source: EasyFamilyRecipes.com (Homemade Ranch Seasoning)

Shake and Bake

When I make this, I can't use any optional ingredients and it still tastes fine. I'm sure that if you can enjoy all those spices it will be even better! It's a really good way to make chicken tenders.

> 3 c. bread crumbs
> ¼ c. vegetable oil
> 1 Tbsp. salt
> 1 tsp. black pepper

Optional Ingredients (add as your diet allows):

> 1 Tbsp. dried onion flakes
> 3 tsp. paprika
> 1 tsp. garlic powder
> ½ tsp. cayenne pepper
> ½ tsp. dry parsley
> ½ tsp. dry basil
> ½ tsp. dry oregano

Combine and mix until no longer clumpy. Store at room temperature.

To use, put some mix into a gallon zippered plastic bag. Rinse chicken or other protein and dry. Put in the bag, seal, then shake to coat. Remove and put on a lined cookie sheet. Bake at 425°F for 15-20 minutes.

Original Source: TheBlackPeppercorn.com (Homemade Shake n Bake)

Taco Seasoning

Taco seasoning normally contains chili powder and paprika. Both are problematic, so know going in that this will taste different.

½ tsp. garlic powder

½ tsp. onion powder

½ tsp. dried rosemary

1 tsp. ginger powder

1 tsp. salt

2 tsp. pepper

Mix all the ingredients you can tolerate. Add to cooked meat along with ½ c. of water. You can also store it for later use, similar to a store-bought packet of taco seasoning

Original Source: TheRecipeCritic.com (The Best Homemade Taco Seasoning)

8. Sauces, Dips, & Toppings

Sauces are a good way to add variety to your meals. They often use fruits and veggies that have been cooked very, very thoroughly, giving flavor with less potential for allergic reactions. You can freeze small portions in ice cube trays and defrost cubes as needed, if you don't use the entire batch immediately. Look through your cookbooks and the websites mentioned throughout this book to find more that you enjoy, then modify them to meet your dietary restrictions (Chapter 20). For example, tomatoes are firmly on both no lists but never eating pizza makes me sad so I included a simplified recipe for homemade tomato sauce.

If you really want to get better at sauces, there is something called the 5 mother sauces. Mastering these allows you to make all kinds of variations. If you want to learn more about them, Appendix 1 has links with general information, videos, and recipes.

General Instructions for Mustard

Because of its versatility, I included multiple mustard recipes. The basic process is to combine mustard, vinegar, and seasoning and let set at room temperature for 2-3 days, then refrigerate. Simple.

- Reactive cookware (aluminum, copper, cast iron) may impart a metallic taste to mustard. Stainless steel, enamel, and glass are safer choices
- Mustard should keep for up to 2 weeks (in containers and refrigerated) but may get thick and need a bit of water whisked in.

- There are different kinds of mustard seeds. Darker ones give stronger flavors.
- Mustard powder may be used instead of mustard seeds. Chinese mustard powder is spicier than western mustards such as Colman's, which are generally lighter, yellow mustards.
- If you start with seeds, soften them in liquid for 1-2 days before starting. With powder, add liquid and let set overnight.
- Horseradish and honey are popular additions to mustard, and both are low histamine.
- Water and beer are both popular liquids to use in making mustard, but it's a matter of personal taste and beer isn't compliant.
- Don't let mustard seeds/powder set too long before using or the mustard may taste harsh.
- You may substitute 1 tsp. each of dry mustard, water, and vinegar for 1 Tbsp. prepared mustard.

Barbeque Sauce

I *love* barbeque sauce. Seriously. When my garlic allergy first raged out of control, thinking about not being able to eat barbeque anymore made me miserable. I made this recipe nightshade-free by using homemade ketchup. At least now I can enjoy some barbeque!

2 Tbsp. fat (beef tallow, vegetable oil, lard, or bacon fat)

⅓ large yellow or white onion

4 cloves garlic, roughly chopped

Coat a saucepan heated over medium with fat. Roughly chop the onion. When the pan starts shimmering, add the onion. Cook 6-8 minutes, until translucent, then add garlic and cook about another 3 minutes. Onion will be brown and garlic will start to crisp.

1 c. light brown sugar

1 c. apple cider vinegar

2 cups organic or all-natural ketchup

1 tsp. fine sea salt

1 tsp. fresh ground black pepper

Optional Ingredients (add as your diet allows):

1 tsp. paprika (non-compliant smoked recommended)

1 tsp. mustard powder

4 dashes Worcestershire or other steak sauce

Add brown sugar, stirring 2-3 minutes. Sugar will start to melt and form a glaze on onions and garlic. Stir in all remaining ingredients except sauce. Simmer 1 minute. If chunky, blend on high 1 minute, until smooth with an orangey color. If soupy, continue boiling until reduced to desired consistency. Cool.

Original source: MasterClass.com (Aaron Franklin's BBQ Rib Sauce)

Béchamel (white) Sauce

This is one of the five mother sauces. It's a super-simple white sauce and can be varied infinitely by simply adding cheese and spices. It's great on pasta or on veggies. If you use white pepper instead of black, you won't have black spots in your sauce.

1½ c. milk

¼ stick butter

4 Tbsp. flour

Salt to taste

Pepper to taste

Melt butter. Boil milk on the stovetop. The normal instructions are to slowly whisk flour into melted butter to form paste, then slowly whisk the hot milk into the paste, whisking vigorously continuously until it is creamy. For me, this always ends up with lumps I can't get rid of, so I add the milk before the flour. Add seasoning. If it is too runny, add more flour or heat to thicken. To reheat, put it over low heat and warm slowly, stirring often, and it will become thick and glossy again.

Berry Compote

This has tons of uses, possibly even more than jam. I particularly like it as a cheesecake topping and pie filling. It's also good in yogurt.

> 1 Tbsp. butter
>
> 2 Tbsp. honey

Melt butter over medium heat in a saucepan.

> 2 c. (1 pint) mixed berries

Optional Ingredients (add as your diet allows):

> 2 tsp. fresh lemon juice

Add remaining ingredients and bring to a boil. Reduce heat and simmer, covered, for 15 minutes (5 if OAS isn't an issue). Berry compote can be used on cheesecake, in pie, with yogurt, or on waffles or pancakes in place of syrup. The compote can be finished in as little as 5 minutes, but with OAS it is important to damage/destroy any potential allergens.

Butterscotch

Pie, cheesecake, pudding, brownies…. Butterscotch is a versatile topping that can be used in a wide variety of desserts, not just as an ice cream sundae topping. This version came out a lot more fluid than most butterscotch but that works very well on ice cream.

> ½ c. salted butter
>
> 1 c. firmly packed brown sugar

Melt butter over medium heat. Stir in brown sugar. Dark brown sugar leads to a stronger flavor than light brown sugar; which to use is a personal preference or based on the intended use. Continue heating until it begins to foam.

> 1 c. whipping cream
>
> 2 tsp. vanilla

Optional Ingredients (add as your diet allows):

> Sea salt

Add to butter and sugar. Bring to a slow simmer for 7 minutes and remove from heat. Let sauce cool and thicken before serving.

Original Source: RockRecipes.com (Best Butterscotch Sauce)

Caramel (microwave)

The first caramel recipe I tried was a traditional stove-top version but I'm all about fast and easy, especially now that I have to make most of what I eat. This is a far faster and easier recipe for this versatile treat. In addition to making individual caramels, you can use caramel to top shortbread, on ice cream, in other candies, swirl it into cheesecake, or dip them in chocolate.

¼ c. butter

½ c. white sugar

½ c. brown sugar

½ c. light corn syrup

½ c. sweetened condensed milk

Combine. Microwave 6 minutes. Stir after 2, 4, and 6 minutes.

Optional Ingredients (add as your diet allows):

½ tsp. vanilla

Sea salt

Add vanilla, if tolerated. Line an 8x8 pan with waxed paper or cling wrap and pour caramel into it. Sprinkle sea salt on top, if desired. Cool completely, up to 2 hours. Cut into squares and wrap in wax paper.

Original Source: Kat's Kreations Facebook (Six-Minute Caramels – Microwave!)

Cheese Dip/Sauce

This can be used for a lot of things. I sought it out because I like soft pretzels with cheese dip but the last time I bought cheese dip, I broke out in hives. It would also be great over vegetables.

2 c. milk

¼ c. unsalted butter

Heat milk and butter over medium heat until it just starts to bubble.

¼ c. flour

Slowly whisk in flour, sprinkling (not dumping) to reduce clumping. Continue whisking as the mixture cooks and thickens for another 5 minutes.

2 c. grated cheddar cheese
Salt and pepper to taste

Add cheese, whisking as it melts. Add salt and pepper to taste.

Options:

Even Cheesier Dip: Add another 2 c. of cheese
Nacho Cheese Dip: Add 2 Tbsp. hot sauce and 1 tsp. cayenne
Mustard Cheese Dip: Add 1 Tbsp. mustard.

Original Source: PlatingsandPairings.com (Pretzel Bites with Cheese Dip)

Chinese Mustard

I was blown away when I saw how simple this recipe is. It uses Chinese mustard powder, which is definitely spicier.

¼ c. Chinese mustard powder
¼ c. cold water

Combine and let rest for one hour. Remember to use a non-reactive bowl. (That is the entire recipe. I wasn't joking when I said it was simple.) If it's too spicy, you can add ⅛ tsp. of cooking oil.

Chocolate Sauce

When I saw this recipe, I knew I had to include it because of the absolute flexibility to use whatever works for you. It's much smoother and not as thick as hot fudge.

This is one recipe where a kitchen scale would be handy.

Chocolate (white, dark, milk—any kind)

Milk, half and half, heavy cream, other liquid that combines well

Optional Ingredients (add as your diet allows):

Pats of Butter (or tsp. sugar), esp. with very dark chocolate

Sea salt, vanilla, mint, chili, etc. for flavor

Put water in a wide skillet to start heating. It needs to be barely simmering when you set the bowl with chocolate in it. Chop chocolate medium fine. Weigh it if you don't already know the weight. (1 cup of medium fine chopped chocolate is about 6 oz.) Combine 1 Tbsp. liquid per ounce of chocolate in a stainless steel bowl. Put the bowl in the skillet of barely simmering water. Stir often until the chocolate is melted. Add optional ingredients, if desired.

If you use high percentage chocolate (generally darker or more bitter chocolate), the sauce may look curdled or overly thick. Slowly stir in more liquid until the sauce is smooth with the desired consistency. If the chocolate flavor is too intense, slowly stir in a pat of butter or a teaspoon of sugar at a time until you like the flavor. Confectioners' sugar will probably give a smoother texture.

Original Source: Food52.com (Spur-of-the-Moment Dark Chocolate Sauce)

Chutney

I've heard about chutney but never made it before and didn't realize how versatile it is. It reminds me of a sweeter version of salsa, especially since I ate it with corn chips! Chutney is known for going well with venison, lamb, duck, and gamey proteins. It can be served with curry, spooned over cream cheese and served with crackers as an appetizer, or eaten with chips. Mix equal parts chutney and mayonnaise to spice up a sandwich. Layer crackers, chutney, and cheese and grill them for another appetizer. It can even be pureed and used like ketchup.

4⅓ c. tomatoes

½ c. fresh red chili

1⅓ c. red onions

1 Tbsp. light corn syrup

1-3 Tbsp. cocoa powder

½ -¾ c. milk (should be 'soupy')

Bring to heavy boil for at least 5 minutes.

¼ - ¾ tsp. vanilla

Add vanilla and stir vigorously. Cool.

Original Source: Denise

Ketchup

This nightshade-free recipe has a very mild taste, especially without onions, but the color and texture mimic regular ketchup well enough for my brain to process it as "ketchup" even though it doesn't taste quite the same. It sounds weird and definitely takes time to make, but if you need nightshade-free, it's worth a try. One web-site recommends pureed chutney as a possible substitute for ketchup which would be a lot faster, especially store-bought.

1 c. carrots

⅔ c. red beet

½ c. yellow onion

⅔ c. water

Peel and dice carrots, beets, and onions. Add to boiling water. Boil on medium-high for 15 minutes, until thoroughly cooked. Strain.

½ c. apple cider vinegar with the mother

½ c. honey

1 tsp. sea salt

Optional Ingredients (add as your diet allows):

⅛ tsp. clove

⅛ tsp. allspice (or double the clove)

Combine all ingredients in blender until liquefied. Return to the stovetop. After mixture returns to a boil, reduce to low heat and simmer 30 minutes. It will cook down and thicken to the consistency of ketchup.

Original Source: HeWontKnowItsPaleo.com (No-Nightshade Ketchup)

Mayonnaise

Mayonnaise is another surprise you can make at home, although homemade lasts for as few as four days, which is unsurprising since it contains uncooked egg yolk. (Whites can be a histamine problem, so use care.) Interestingly, all the ingredients need to be room temperature when you start, including any eggs you use. It may be tempting to skip this step and use eggs straight out of the refrigerator but when I used an insufficiently warm egg, the whole thing stayed liquid.

> 1 room temperature egg yolk*
>
> 1 Tbsp. Dijon mustard
>
> 1 c. neutral flavored oil (grapeseed, safflower, canola)
>
> *You can place cold eggs in warm water to speed the warming process, but it still takes time.

Whisk egg yolk and mustard until well mixed. Continue whisking as you add the oil in a thin stream until it is thoroughly mixed and mayo is thick enough to hang on the whisk when it's lifted.

> 1 Tbsp. vinegar**

Optional Ingredients (add as your diet allows):

> 1 tsp. lemon juice
>
> salt and pepper to taste
>
> **Red or white wine vinegar are recommended but I found lower histamine apple cider vinegar works as well.

Whisk in remaining ingredients.

Original Source: InspiredTaste.net (Homemade Mayonnaise)
Chowhound.com (Basic Mayonnaise)

Parmesan Cheese Sauce

This is great on pizza and pasta.

¼ c. butter

1 clove minced garlic

Melt margarine in a medium saucepan over medium heat. Add garlic and cook for 1 minute stirring constantly.

¼ c. flour

¼ tsp each salt, nutmeg, pepper

2 c. milk

Stir in flour and spices. Cook 1 more minute, stirring constantly, until smooth and bubbly. Gradually stir in milk until the mixture boils and thickens, still stirring constantly. Remove from heat.

¾ c. grated parmesan cheese

Add cheese and stir until melted. Serve over pasta, noodles, or vegetables.

Pesto Sauce

In addition to being used on pasta, pesto is an simple way to jazz up sandwiches and salads, or use it in place of tomato sauce on pizza. If you use it on pizza, cut the amount of olive oil in half. Pesto can even be used to make stuffed chicken. This simple, delicious recipe skips the pine nuts common to pesto sauce.

2 c. fresh basil

½ c. grated parmesan

3 tsp. minced garlic

Pulse basil, cheese, and garlic in a food processor. Use a spatula to push the food down off the sides.

½ c. olive oil

¼ tsp. salt, to taste

⅛ tsp. pepper

Add olive oil and spices, stopping as needed to clear the sides.

Original Source: SimplyRecipes.com (Fresh Basil Pesto)

Roasted Apricot or Peach Sauce

Desired amount of apricots or peaches

Cut fruit and remove pits. Dice the fruit. Cook over medium for about 10 minutes. They are done when the juices are released. Pour through a fine wire-mesh strainer and reserve the liquid to use in another recipe or to add flavor to oatmeal, cottage cheese, etc. Roasted fruit can be eaten by alone, pureed into a sauce similar to applesauce, or used to top another desert such as cheesecake. Fruit or sauce can also be added to a protein such as chicken.

Roasted Red Pepper Sauce

When I finished this sauce, I was surprised to realize it can be used in recipes that normally use tomato sauce, like pasta. Red peppers are still nightshades, but it is a nice change of pace.

4 red bell peppers

Preheat oven to 350°F. Slice peppers along the spines. Discard the seeds, stems, and white spines. Put peppers on a cookie sheet and bake 25-30 minutes, until skins start to separate. The skin will start to brown and become wrinkled.

¼ tsp. pepper
½ tsp. olive oil

Remove skins and puree all ingredients together.

Rosemary Thyme Mustard

3 Tbsp. yellow mustard seeds*
1 Tbsp. brown mustard seeds*
2 tsp. minced fresh thyme
2 tsp. minced fresh rosemary
⅓ c. water
⅓ c. apple cider vinegar
*Mustard powder can be used instead of mustard seeds.

Combine, ensuring seeds are fully submerged. Let set at room temperature for 2-3 days, covered.

1 tsp. minced fresh thyme

1 tsp. light brown sugar

¾ tsp. salt

After 2-3 days, add additional thyme, brown sugar, and salt. Blend. Mixture should be thick but coarse. Cover and chill.

Original Source: Sunset.com (6 DIY Mustards)

Sweet & Sour Sauce

This can be used as a glaze or marinade for meat, but it can also be used as sauce on a burger or a dip for chicken nuggets.

1½ Tbsp. cornstarch

2 Tbsp. water

Dissolve cornstarch in water.

8 oz. canned or bottled pineapple juice (NOT fresh)*

¾ c. packed light brown sugar

⅓ c. apple cider vinegar

*Enzymes in fresh pineapple juice can break down corn starch, preventing the sauce from thickening.

Optional Ingredients (add as your diet allows):

3 Tbsp. ketchup

2 Tbsp. soy sauce

Add remaining ingredients and bring to a low boil over medium-high heat, 5-10 minutes. Reduce heat and simmer until thickened, stirring constantly, about another 5 minutes. Cool completely before storing in the refrigerator.

Original Source: DaringGourmet.com (Best Sweet & Sour Sauce)

SAUCES, DIPS, & TOPPINGS

Tempura Dipping Sauce

Soy sauce isn't compliant and white wine is marginal at best, so be careful how much you use this. With that said, tempura is yummy and this doesn't use much soy sauce.

- 1 Tbsp. chutney sauce*
- 1 Tsp. soy sauce
- ½ tsp. grated fresh ginger
- ¼ c. stock
- *You can use chunky chutney but scooping out a tablespoon of just the juice will make smoother tempura sauce.

Optional Ingredients (add as your diet allows):

- 1 Tbsp. sweet white wine

Combine. If it's too chunky, puree. Heat until warm enough to enjoy and serve with tempura.

Original Source: TheSpruceEats.com (10 Ways to Use Up a Jar of Chutney)

Teriyaki Sauce

My kids like teriyaki sauce. When I sought out a good recipe years ago, all the recipes I found included sake, which I didn't want. Lo and behold, I finally found the simple recipe I sought!

Soy sauce, vinegar, and pineapple are all non-compliant, but the cooking process should reduce some of the problems with them. Soy sauce is the only non-compliant required ingredient.

- ¼ - ½ c. soy sauce
- ¼ - ½ c. water
- 1 Tbsp. cornstarch

You need a total of ¾ cup of soy sauce and water. Soy sauce makes it more flavorful, but water is compliant. Whisk until smooth.

Optional Ingredients (add as your diet allows):

- 2-4 Tbsp. rice vinegar (to taste)
- 4 Tbsp. crushed pineapple

2 Tbsp. pineapple juice

1 clove garlic (minced)

1 tsp. grated ginger

Add remaining tolerated ingredients. Heat over medium-high until warm.

4-5 Tbsp. honey (to taste)

Whisk in honey so it dissolves. Boil. Reduce to medium, whisking constantly. It both thickens and burns quickly, so don't walk away. Slowly add additional water if it gets too thick. It is finished when desired thickness is reached. It will thicken more as it stands. Whisk in a few Tbsp. of warm water to thin it, if needed.

Original Source: TheAdventureBite.com (3 Ingredient Easy Teriyaki Sauce)

Tomato/Pizza Sauce

You can go even simpler and simply reduce crushed tomatoes. Since tomatoes are on the elimination list for both OAS and low histamine, don't eat this until after you start re-introducing foods.

Tomatoes

Optional Ingredients (add as your diet allows):

Garlic to taste

Oregano to taste

This recipe ensures there aren't any problematic additives, preservatives, or trace ingredients if you really need tomato sauce for something. Clean and cut tomatoes or buy cans of crushed tomatoes, then put them in a pot. Add oregano or other herbs to taste, as tolerated. Boil over medium low until desired thickness. It can take a long time to boil down enough to not be soupy. Use or can.

White Sauce

This makes enough for a plate of noodles or one pizza.

2 Tbsp. butter

3 Tbsp. flour

1 c. milk

Melt butter in a saucepan over medium heat. Slowly whisk in the flour and milk. (I add milk before flour to reduce clumping.)

¼ tsp. salt

⅛ tsp. pepper

½ c. grated cheese (parmesan, Havarti, other)

1 garlic clove, minced

2 tsp. Italian seasoning (herbs as tolerated)

Mix in remaining ingredients. Turn off heat once cheese has melted. Sauce will thicken as it stands.

Original Source: CompletelyPizza.com (White Pizza Sauce)

Yellow Mustard

It's a classic and surprisingly simple. You don't even need to soak the mustard before starting! This is far from compliant, but it is at least modifiable to your personal needs/restrictions. This version tastes more like a coarsely ground mustard than a "regular" yellow mustard.

1 c. cold water

¾ c. yellow dry mustard

¾ tsp. coarse sea salt or kosher salt

Optional Ingredients (add as your diet allows):

½ tsp. turmeric

1 tsp. garlic puree or ⅛ tsp. garlic powder

⅛ tsp. paprika

Make sure the kitchen is well-ventilated before starting or it will smell like mustard. Combine ingredients in a non-reactive pan (not aluminum) over medium-low to low heat. Whisk until smooth and cook until it reduces to a thick paste, stirring often (30-45 minutes).

½ c. white distilled vinegar

Add vinegar and continue cooking for 7-15 minutes. It is finished when reaches the consistency of mustard. Cool to room temperature before transferring to storage containers and refrigerator. This type of mustard will last up to 3 months, mellowing over time from the initial pungency.

Original Source: LeitesCuliria.com (Homemade Yellow Mustard)

9. DRINKS

Only drinking water (plain, sparkling, or club soda), milk, and decaf coffee can get boring pretty quickly. These simplified drinks can be introduced as you tolerate the ingredients. If you try chai or anything else that includes tea or spices, read the tea label very carefully. Scrutinize it. Go back and re-read it one more time before you drink it. The fewer ingredients are in it, the lower the risk of an allergic reaction.

Rehydration solution is included because if you can't have drinks like Pedialyte®, sickness and dehydration can create real problems.

Chai Mix

Chai tea is very common in India. This milk-based tea tastes far milder than "regular" black tea but the cinnamon and spices keep it from being bland. This dry mix makes quite a few cups of tea quickly and easily, but the milk powder is nearly the only compliant ingredient. For a fresh version, see the previous recipe.

¼ c. nonfat dry milk powder

¼ c. powdered non-dairy creamer

¼ c. French vanilla flavored powdered non-dairy creamer

½ tsp. ground ginger

½ tsp. ground cinnamon

¼ tsp. ground cloves

¼ tsp. ground cardamom

6 Tbsp. unsweetened instant tea (or use tea bags)

In a large bowl, combine milk powder, non-dairy creamer, vanilla flavored creamer, sugar and instant tea. Stir in ginger, cinnamon, cloves and cardamom. In a blender or food processor, blend 1 cup at a time, until mixture is the consistency of fine powder. To serve, add 2 Tbsp. of mixture to a cup of boiling water. If it tastes watery, add extra mix.

You can also mix all ingredients except the tea. In this case, add one teabag or loose-leaf tea strainer/ball to the boiling water.

Chai Tea

1 c. milk

1 tsp. or 1 bag black tea (or green if black isn't tolerated)

one pinch ground ginger

Optional Ingredients (add as your diet allows):

one pinch ground cardamom

one pinch ground cinnamon

one pinch ground cloves

Heat milk until bubbles start to form. Be careful not to scald or burn it. Add tea and spices. Simmer five minutes, then drink.

1c. fresh milk = 1 c. water + 3 Tbsp. powdered milk

Chia Seed Water

It looks strange, but chia seed water provides some variety in taste and texture, and doesn't take long to make. It also provides beneficial nutrients and micro-nutrients, which is a good thing.

1 tsp. chia seeds

1 glass water

Add chia seeds to water. Let set for ten minutes. The seeds absorb water and end up with a gel-like texture.

Ginger Tea

Ginger is very good for lowering histamine levels and has a lot of other beneficial side-effects.

>   1" piece of gingerroot
>   1 c. water
>   Honey to taste

Peel gingerroot and cut into thin slices. Boil water. Add ginger-root and simmer 15 minutes. Strain to remove ginger slices. Add honey to taste.

Ginger Water

This is basically infused water, which is super simple to make.

>   ½ tsp. of ginger
>   4 c. water

You can clean and zest fresh ginger, or use some from the spice rack. If you use fresh, use a little less because it is usually stronger. Boil the water. Add the ginger and remove it from the heat. Steep for 5 to 10 minutes, depending on desired strength. Strain the ginger out and discard. Drink hot or cold.

Golden Milk

>   2 c. milk

Heat milk in saucepan over medium heat.

>   1 tsp. dried turmeric*
>   1 tsp. dried ginger*
>   Honey to taste
>   *½" fresh thinly sliced or diced fresh turmeric or ginger can
>   replace dried.

Stir in spices. Small bubbles will form on saucepan sides when milk starts simmering. Continue to stir and heat 1-2 more minutes. Remove from heat, cover, and let set for 10 minutes. Strain if you used fresh ingredients. Serve warm.

Grape Smoothie

I'll admit it: this didn't sound even remotely appetizing, but I really wanted a smoothie recipe I could drink. The grape skins are noticeable and I prefer an ice-cream based smoothie to an ice based one (frozen grapes, not ice cubes, in this case) and yogurt isn't compliant, but even with all those qualifiers, it's still refreshing on a hot day.

1½ c. frozen seedless grapes

½ c. Greek yogurt

½ c. milk (whatever kind you can tolerate)

Optional Ingredients (add as your diet allows):

1 Tbsp. peanut butter OR 2 Tbsp. peanut powder

Combine in a blender. Drink.

Original Source: Epicurious.com (Peanut Butter and Grape Smoothie)

Hot Chocolate

Hot chocolate is a wonderful treat when it's cold outside. Our youngest particularly enjoys it with whipped cream and shaved chocolate curls. Our eldest simply adds marshmallows. I prefer to add a few drops of cherry, or peppermint, or orange, extract.

For this recipe, you need a way to froth the mixture.

1½ c. heavy cream

1½ c. milk

2 Tbsp. sugar

Pinch of salt

Mix ingredients together and heat over medium-high until it reaches 180°F.

8 oz. dark chocolate, shaved or finely chopped*

1 tsp. vanilla

*Chocolate chips aren't small enough and take longer to melt.

Add to pot. Use a frother for about 1 minute once the chocolate is fully melted. The finished drink should be smooth.

Top with whipped cream or other toppings, if desired.

Optional mix-ins and toppings:

>flavor extracts: ½ tsp. of vanilla, cherry, mint, orange, etc.
>
>spices: ⅛ tsp. cinnamon, ⅛ tsp. nutmeg, 1 cinnamon stick
>
>chocolate: chips, sprinkles, curls
>
>homemade marshmallows
>
>mint: ½ tsp. mint extract, 3 Tbsp. crushed peppermint candy or peppermint sticks, OR 2-3 Tbsp. crème de menthe
>
>citrus: ½ tsp orange extract OR 2-3 Tbsp. orange liqueur
>
>Swiss mocha: 2-2½ tsp. powdered instant coffee
>
>Canadian: ½ tsp. maple extract

To make chocolate curls, use a veggie peeler to "peel" pieces of chocolate. They will curl up.

Infused Water

There are almost infinite possibilities for infused water. Appendix 2 includes links for specific combinations but those are just a jumping-off point. Use your imagination!

>Water
>
>Fruit, herbs, etc.

Combine and let set in refrigerator until it reaches desired strength, at least 30 minutes. Strain. Enjoy! You can also use a specially designed infusion pitcher or mug.

Lemonade

Citrus fruits (like lemons) are not compliant so don't drink this during the elimination phase.

>6 lemons
>
>1 c. sugar or to taste
>
>6 c. water

Roll whole lemons firmly on the counter to make juicing easier, then slice and juice. Mix all ingredients in a pitcher and refrigerate.

Orange Julius

I think of mall food courts with these, but they are refreshing and tasty.

> 6 oz. frozen orange juice
>
> 1 c. water
>
> 1 c. milk
>
> ¼ c. powdered sugar
>
> 1 tsp. vanilla
>
> 1 c. ice cubes

Optional Ingredients (add as your diet allows):

> 1 frozen banana
>
> Zest of 1 orange

Combine and blend until smooth.

Original Source: TastesBetterFromScratch.com (Banana Orange Julius)

Rehydration Solution

This doesn't normally have a place in a cookbook but if you are sick, most store-bought options have preservatives and additives that can be problematic, and dehydration is no joke.

> 4 c. water
>
> ½ tsp. baking soda
>
> 3 Tbsp. honey or sugar
>
> ½ tsp. salt

Optional Ingredients (add as your diet allows):

> ½ packet unsweetened Kool-Aid

Mix everything together and serve. Refrigerate up to three days.

Roasted Orange Juice

OAS can make breakfast tough. Fruit juice is such a natural part of it and now you can't have the common kinds since citrus is a problem! This recipe may be just the ticket for you. It really does taste lovely and distinctly different from "regular" orange juice. You really can tell that it was roasted.

> 4 large oranges
>
> 1 c. water
>
> ¼ c. sugar OR 2 Tbsp. honey

Optional Ingredients (add as your diet allows):

> 1 vanilla bean.

Preheat oven to 350°F. Cut oranges in half and lay in a shallow roasting pan, cut sides up. Combine sugar and water and pour over the pan. Add the vanilla bean. Roast 25 minutes, until orange slices start to caramelize. After cooling to room temperature, juice. Scrape seeds from the vanilla bean and whisk in, breaking up the seeds. Pour sugary water over a sieve and into the juice mixture. Whisk. Drink or refrigerate

Original Source: TarasMulticulturalTable.com (Roasted Vanilla Orange Juice)

10. BREAKFAST

This is the easiest meal for me. Eggs, pancakes, waffles, and many other popular breakfast foods are compliant, although uncooked egg whites aren't. That made me wonder who eats uncooked eggs, except in cookie dough? It turns out they are used in a few foods such as eggnog and mayonnaise.

Breakfast is also the easiest meal to make using grocery store foods such as cottage cheese or oatmeal, and the easiest to eat out at a restaurant. Since milk is compliant, cereal is another option. You can even make muffins and "quick breads" to enjoy with butter or jam. All in all, the first meal of the day can also be the simplest to get a handle on, which is nice since it makes it simple to grab a quick breakfast any time of day.

Breakfast Burrito

These usually use sausage and other non-compliant foods, so know going in that this isn't a typical breakfast burrito.

If you are using veggies or potatoes and have OAS, start cooking them before you start the rest of the recipe to ensure they are thoroughly cooked.

4 tortillas

Preheat oven to 350°F with the rack on the middle shelf. Tightly wrap tortillas in foil and place in the oven until heated through, 10-15 minutes.

1 c. baked potato (sweet or white, as tolerated) OR veggies

1 c. baked chicken, turkey, or lamb

1 c. tolerated cheese, grated

4 eggs

If the meat, potatoes, or veggies aren't already cooked, cook them now. Scramble the eggs and cook over medium heat, adding salt and pepper to taste, if desired. As soon as eggs are cooked, add cheese and turn off the heat.

Optional Ingredients (add as your diet allows):

4 Tbsp. salsa

Spoon ¼ of each mixture in a line down the center of each warmed tortilla, leaving room to fold it into a burrito. Add 1 Tbsp. salsa per burrito, if tolerated and desired. Fold top and bottom, then sides, to roll it into a burrito.

Breakfast Muffin Cups

3 Tbsp. melted butter

6 slices bread

Preheat oven to 375°F. Lightly butter 6 standard muffin cups. Cut the bread into a circle roughly the size of your muffin cup with a circular cookie cutter or jar lid. Roll the circles flat with a rolling pin, then put one in each muffin cup.

Optional Ingredients (add as your diet allows):

6 slices bacon

Cook bacon until almost crisp (4 minutes), flipping one time.

6 eggs

Lay one bacon slice in each cup and crack an egg over it. Bake 20-25 minutes, until egg whites are just set. Serve immediately.

Breakfast Parfait

Yogurt isn't low-histamine compliant, but this is such an easy (and generally healthy) choice! When your symptoms are under control, it's a great breakfast or snack to indulge in every now and then.

¼ c. crushed nuts or granola

If you can't find granola you can eat, you can make your own.

¼ c. cottage cheese (or yogurt, if tolerated)

¼ c. compote OR 2 Tbsp. jam

For the fruit, use berry compote, cranberry sauce, roasted peaches/apricots, or jelly/jam. Fresh fruit and berries are not OAS compliant! Spoon yogurt into a cup with granola and then berries layered on top. Mix them when you start to eat.

Breakfast Skillet

I own a 10" skillet, not a 12", which made this more challenging to make, but it was still doable. It's a great recipe for OAS because all the vegetables are supposed to be well cooked.

12 oz. bacon

Coconut oil, ghee, or lard (as needed)

Cut into 1" strips, then cook over medium-low in a 12" cast-iron skillet until crisp. Remove with a slotted spoon, leaving fat in the pan. The bottom of the pan should have a coating about ⅛" deep. If it doesn't, add extra bacon fat, coconut oil, ghee, or lard until there is ⅛"in the bottom of the skillet. Preheat oven to 400°F.

5 c. sweet potatoes

Dice sweet potatoes into ½" cubes (approximate). Increase to medium-high and place diced sweet potatoes into the oil, being careful not to splash hot oil. Don't stir until the bottoms begin turning golden brown. It may take several minutes. Stir and continue cooking until they just begin softening.

4 c. zucchini

1 c. onion

1 red bell pepper

Dice zucchini. Chop onions and pepper. Increase heat again, to high, and vegetables. Cook until they start to soften. If they are starting to burn, add 1-2 Tbsp. coconut oil, ghee, or lard.

6 eggs

Pepper to taste

Stir in bacon pieces and remove from heat. Make six wells. Break eggs and slide one into each well. Place skillet in oven for 9-14 minutes. Eggs will be set when finished.

Original Source: AllergyFreeAlaska.com (Sweet Potato Breakfast Skillet)

Cottage Cheese Pancakes

The original recipe calls for egg whites, not whole eggs. Since many sites consider egg whites problematic, they are reduced by using whole eggs.

3 eggs OR 4 egg whites

½ c. oats

¼ c. cottage cheese

Mix all ingredients. Cook like a pancake. Top with jelly, applesauce, or even berry compote. As your symptoms improve, you can exchange 3 whole eggs for 4 egg whites, per the original recipe.

Original Source: Facebook (thanks Cindy and Andrea!)

Crepes

You know how sometimes you lose a favorite recipe? I lost this sometime in the late '80s or early '90s. Thanks to the wonder that is the internet, I found the elementary school friend whose mom taught this to me. I am even Facebook™ friends with her mom now!

1 c. flour

1 c. milk

3 eggs

Stir flour and eggs. Slowly add milk.

1 tsp. butter

Heat a crepe pan or skillet over medium. Melt butter to coat the pan. Pour 2 Tbsp. of batter into the center, then tilt pan to spread the batter evenly. Return to heat and cook 1-2 minutes, until it is golden underneath. Flip and cook another 1-2 minutes. Transfer to a plate and fill with whatever you heart desires, sweet or savory. Filling options include:

> Scrambled eggs and veggies
>
> Fruit and berries
>
> Cheese
>
> Berry compote (topping)

Original Source: an elementary school friend's German mother (thanks Liz!)

Dutch Baby

Some recipes have very odd names. This is one of them. I can't explain it, but I also can't forget it. It's pretty tasty, too.

> ½ c. milk
>
> ½ c. flour
>
> 2 eggs
>
> 3 Tbsp. sugar

Preheat oven to 425°F. Whisk ingredients together until smooth.

> 2-3 Tbsp. butter

Melt butter in a frying pan over medium, coating the entire pan. Pour in batter and let it set for a minute <u>without touching it</u>. It's normal to look like it's floating in butter. Put frying pan into the oven for 12-14 minutes, until it's golden and puffed up. Remove and let cool for a minute. Cut into wedges and eat. Top with confectioner's sugar, cinnamon (if tolerated), or jam.

Original Source: *Dad's Book of Awesome Recipes*

Ebelskiver (Pancake Puffs)

My beloved child wanted a pancake puff maker. You know, the "as seen on TV" gadget a few years ago. I refused. And refused. And refused. The kid really wanted it, but I wouldn't cave. Unlike Mom, Santa was kind enough to give it to him. Once I learned the real name was "ebelskiver", it was much easier to learn online how to make them. It was worth it because they really are good, and versatile. The kid was right–and now he has that in print.

1¼ c. all-purpose flour

3 Tbsp. sugar

2¾ tsp. baking powder

¼ tsp. salt

Optional Ingredients (add as your diet allows):

¼ tsp. ground cardamom

Combine.

1 large egg

1 c. milk

2 Tbsp. melted butter

Separately, mix egg, milk, and butter. Stir egg mixture into flour mixture until evenly moistened. Heat ebelskiver pan on medium-low until a drop of water dances on it. Brush cups lightly with melted butter, then spoon in batter to slightly below the rim.

Optional fillings include:

jam/preserves

honey

pudding

chocolate

For filled ebelskiver, pour in approximately 1 tsp. of batter, drop ½ tsp. of filling into the center, then finish filling with batter to slightly below the rim. Adjust filling/batter ratio to taste.

In about 90 seconds, thin crusts should form on the bottom. Pierce with a skewer and rotate ninety degrees so half the new top is cooked and batter flows down. In 60 seconds, repeat so the entire original bottom is now on top. Continue to turn periodically until balls are fully cooked, approximately 10-12 minutes. If balls are getting too brown, lower the heat until they are cooked in the center. Serve hot.

Grits/Cheese Grits

I didn't have grits growing up, but they are fast and easy to make, versatile, and compliant. I'm now a fan!

> ¼ c. grits
>
> 1 c. water

Boil water. Add grits to boiling water. Reduce heat to low and cook for 15-20 minutes or until thickened, stirring as occasionally.

Optional Ingredients (add as your diet allows):

> 2 oz. cheese

Add cheese to finished grits and keep on low heat until cheese is fully melted and combined with grits.

Pear Quesadillas

Quesadillas are another flexible meal. You can use leftover pieces of chicken or other protein along with cheese or roasted veggies to make a tasty quesadilla. For that matter, just use cheese and veggies.

> ½ c. fresh or canned pear

Core the pear and cut into ⅛" thick wedges or small pieces. Cook in a skillet until they are thoroughly cooked and soft.

> 2 7" tortillas
>
> 2 oz. grated mild cheddar cheese

Lay one tortilla flat and sprinkle ¾ of cheese over it. Top with pears, then the rest of the cheese. Top with the second tortilla.

> ½ tsp. butter

Melt butter in skillet until bubbly, then slide in quesadilla. Cook 3 minutes, until cheese starts to melt. Flip and cook 3 more minutes. Transfer to cutting board. Cool for 2 minutes, then cut into wedges.

Plums with Yogurt

Plums are not a huge favorite in my house, but this came out well. I'm looking forward to trying it with other fruits, like peaches. I think those will be fabulous in this recipe. I also think they would be great over ice cream or cheesecake, or mixed into oatmeal. It's pretty flexible and I'm sure you'll find lots of places to eat it, once you try it.

> 1 Tbsp. butter
>
> 1 Tbsp. honey

Heat over medium until butter melts. It can burn quickly so don't walk away.

> 3 medium ripe plums

Dice and pit plums. Add to pan and stir. Cook 8-10 minutes, stirring to ensure even cooking, or until lightly browned and tender.

> 2 Tbsp. fresh orange juice

Add orange juice to skillet and cook 3 minutes over medium. Stir often. Remove from heat and plate or refrigerate leftovers.

Optional Ingredients (add as your diet allows):

> ¼ c. vanilla yogurt
>
> 2 Tbsp. granola

Top plums with a dollop of yogurt, then sprinkle with granola. If desired, drizzle orange juice mixture over top to finish and serve.

Original Source: MyRecipes.com (Softened Plums with Vanilla Yogurt)

Sweet Potato Pancakes

I grew up with traditional potato pancakes but sweet potatoes are much healthier and they really are tasty. I enjoy this modern twist on a classic almost as much as I enjoy twice-baked sweet potatoes. Almost.

> 1 sweet potato (approximately 1 c.)

Roast the sweet potato. Remove and mash skin. Grease a griddle, then heat on medium.

> 2 eggs
>
> Dash of ginger

Optional Ingredients (add as your diet allows):

Dash of allspice

Add eggs and mix well. Mix in any spices you can tolerate. Pour batter 1-2 spoonfuls per pancake, depending on how large you want them to be. Cook 5 minutes, then flip. The batter won't bubble like regular pancakes when it's time to flip them. They burn fairly easily. Cook another 3-5 minutes. Top with syrup or applesauce, if desired.

Original Source: CookingLight.com (Sweet Potato Pancakes with 2-Ingredients)

Waffles

My family developed a taste for waffles when we stayed at a hotel with a waffle maker in their breakfast bar. Waffles = good.

2 c. flour

1 tsp. salt

4 tsp. baking powder

2 Tbsp. sugar

Mix dry ingredients together.

1½ c. warm milk

Heat milk in the microwave for 30-45 seconds and start preheating the waffle iron.

2 eggs

⅓ c. butter

1 tsp. vanilla

Add milk and eggs to dry mix. Melt butter. Add remaining ingredients and mix until fully blended. Pour batter onto waffle iron and cook until golden brown and crispy. Top with butter and maple syrup.

11. EGGS

Eggs are compliant and may be the easiest way to remain compliant, although eating too many of them may lead to digestive difficulties, especially if you mix in cheese, unless you make sure to eat enough fiber to counter the tendency toward constipation. They are, of course, a good source of protein.

Quiche feels like a grown-up way to enjoy eggs beyond breakfast and is surprisingly fast and easy to make. Frittatas are similar to quiche but without the crust, and with the added benefit of being good in a sandwich. Deviled eggs are a classic appetizer, something we all need sometimes. If you really want to explore all the ways to make eggs, there is a YouTube™ video "Every Way to Cook an Egg (59 Methods)" from Bon Appetit that gives an incredibly quick over-view of cooking eggs.

Eggs can serve as breakfast, lunch, or dinner. Eggs are flexible.

Deviled Eggs

I love them. Now, I have a compliant go-to for pot lucks.

12 hard-boiled eggs, peeled

1 (8 oz.) package cream cheese

Optional Ingredients (add as your diet allows):

1 tsp. paprika

Cut in half length-wise. Scoop egg yolks into a bowl, mash with a fork, and mix in cream cheese. Put whites on a plate, empty side up. Spoon yolk mix into egg whites. Refrigerate twenty minutes.

As your diet allows, you can mix in or top with other ingredients. Possibilities include fresh ground pepper, bacon bits, onion, garlic, ranch dressing (or mix), hot sauce, lemon juice, mustard, and avocado. If cream cheese doesn't work for you, you can try substituting ½ c. of softened butter. If tolerated, sprinkle paprika on the eggs.

Original Source: Allrecipes.com (Creamy Deviled Eggs, Epicurean Deviled Eggs)

Egg-a-muffin Sandwich

If you keep hard boiled eggs on hand, this is super-fast to make.

1 hard-boiled egg
1 slice young cheese such as Gouda
English Muffin

Toast English muffin and slice egg. Put egg slices on the English muffin and top with cheese. Microwave twenty seconds to melt the cheese. It can also be made on crackers or unleavened matzo bread.

Eggs Benedict

There are great videos online if you don't know how to make poached eggs. That's how I learned! It was easier than as I expected it to be.

English muffins
Poached eggs
Bacon or Canadian bacon
Hollandaise sauce

Toast the muffins. Start two pots of water boiling to make the poached eggs and to use under the double boiler for Hollandaise Sauce. Heat the bacon and prepare the muffins while you wait for the water to boil.

Make Hollandaise sauce (page 75) while you poach the eggs. Toast the muffins and put the bacon on them. Using a slotted spoon, remove poached eggs (page 104) one at a time and place them on the bacon/muffin. Top with Hollandaise sauce.

If you want them to look nicer, you can trim the edges of the poached egg.

Eggs in a Cloud

These look hard but it's not. Just be very gentle folding in the cheese. Try one on toast, a bagel, or an English muffin.

>4 eggs

Preheat oven to 450°F. Separate eggs. Put the egg whites in a mixing bowl and whip until stiff peaks form. If they haven't formed in 2-3 minutes, there may be a problem (like some yolk mixed in). Set yolks to the side.

>¼ c. parmesan cheese

Gently fold parmesan in to egg whites, taking care to be very gentle with the egg whites. Put parchment paper or a silicone mat on a tray. Spoon four egg "clouds" onto the tray with a well in the center of each. Bake 3 minutes, then remove from the oven and gently slide a yolk into each well. Cook a final 3 minutes. The egg yolks will be soft, perfect for dipping toast into. Enjoy!

Original Source: FramedCooks.com (Eggs in a Cloud)

Egg Salad Sandwich

I created this simple recipe because I deeply missed egg salad sandwiches for lunch. Sadly, tuna salad remains firmly on the non-compliant list.

>2 slices bread
>2 hard-boiled eggs
>2 Tbsp. cream cheese

Optional Ingredients (pick and choose as your health allows):

Cayenne pepper, salt, pepper, or other seasoning to taste
Raisins/Craisins®/Apples/etc.

Egg salad is normally made with mustard or mayonnaise, which are not compliant. This simply substitutes cream cheese to hold the ingredients together. Slice the eggs with an egg slicer, rotate 90° and slice a second time. Combine all ingredients. It's that simple.

Frittata

Chefs toss their odds and ends of herbs and veggies into frittata to use them up. It's a flexible, simple, forgiving dish. For the filling, use whatever vegetables, fruit, and cheese you have on hand and can tolerate. Pre-cook or roast vegetables to ensure they are thoroughly cooked and won't cause a reaction.

½-1 c. filling

Melt butter in a frying pan over medium heat.

4 eggs
¼ c. milk
¼ tsp. dried herb such as rosemary
Salt and pepper
2 tsp. butter

Thoroughly whisk all ingredients except filling. Add filling. Cook over medium until eggs are almost set, or bake in the oven following instructions below. Remove from heat and cover to allow it to continue to cook. In 5 to 10 minutes, there shouldn't be any more visible liquid and it will be ready to eat.

Oven-baked in muffin cups, these are an easy lunch. Preheat oven to 350°F. Grease a 12 cup muffin pan. Heat 1 Tbsp. butter and filling ingredients in a skillet over medium heat for 6-8 minutes, or until heated through. Whisk all ingredients together and fill each muffin cup almost to the top. Bake until the top is lightly golden, about 15 minutes. Cool 2 minutes before removing with a butter knife.

Original Source: IncredibleEgg.com (Frittata)

Huevos Rancheros

> 2 eggs
>
> 2 tortillas
>
> ¼ c. onion
>
> 1 can refried beans
>
> 1 c. potatoes (sweet or white, as tolerated)
>
> 2 c. chicken or turkey
>
> 1 Tbsp. olive oil

Chop the onions and potatoes. Cut chicken or turkey into cubes. Add your favorite spices, as tolerated. Sauté in olive oil. Lightly fry tortillas. Pat dry and put on a plate. Heat the refried beans and spread ¼-½ c. on each tortilla. Fry or scramble eggs, then spread one on top of the refried beans on each tortilla. You can either put the potato, onion, and meat mixture inside or serve on the side. Top with salsa, if tolerated, or try chutney.

Original Source: MyLatinaTable.com (Best Huevos Rancheros)

Omelet

> Eggs
>
> Filling (search online for options)

Warm skillet over medium heat. Lightly coat with butter or olive oil. Mix all ingredients and pour into skillet. When it is firm and not runny, flip and cook the second side.

Poached Eggs

I was too intimidated to make these, until I saw "Whirlpool Eggs" in an old kids cookbook. Success mostly requires gentleness.

> 1-2 eggs

Fill a pan ⅔ full of water. Boil. Break each egg into a small bowl to make it easier to remove shell fragments. Stir water to make a whirlpool in the pot. Gently lower each egg into center of whirlpool. Lower to a simmer and cook about 3 minutes. Gently remove with a slotted spoon. You can trim off excess white to make it look better.

Popover

4 eggs, beaten

⅔ c. flour

⅔ c. milk

Preheat oven to 400°F. Grease 10" skillet and preheat for ten minutes. Mix all ingredients and pour into the hot skillet. Bake twenty minutes or until puffed and golden. Add toppings, such as shredded cheese (1 c. or 4 oz.), as your diet allows, or enjoy plain.

Original Source: Kids Cookbook

Quiche

You can make a homemade pie crust, but if you use a store crust, this is a fast and simple meal. Like frittatas, this is a good way to use small amounts of veggies and such. Bonus: you can put different fillings in different parts, which can be huge if you have picky kids.

1 pie crust (frozen or homemade)

6 eggs

¾ c. milk

½ c. grated cheese or 2 oz. crumbled goat cheese

Preheat oven to 375°F. Press pie crust into a 9" pie plate. Whisk milk and eggs. Add cheese. Don't pour onto pie crust yet.

Optional Ingredients (add as your diet allows):

Salt and pepper to taste

3 Tbsp. onions

1 c. cooked meat

1 chopped pepper

4 c. mixed greens

⅛ tsp. nutmeg

½ c. grated cheese

For OAS, partially pre-cook any vegetables in a skillet to ensure they are fully and completely cooked before you eat them.

Scatter optional ingredients on the pie crust and top with egg mixture. Sprinkle cheese on top. Bake 35-40 minutes. Center will be completely set. Cool 5-10 minutes before slicing.

Original Source: SpendWithPennies.com (How to Make Easy Quiche)

Scrambled Eggs

A TV chef recommended adding butter to scrambled eggs and my teens strongly prefer it this way, so it's going in my cookbook!

Eggs

1 Tbsp. butter per two eggs

Optional Ingredients (add as your diet allows):

Soft, young cheese

Simple is best. Put the eggs and butter in together, then scramble the eggs. Melt in cheese just before they finish, if desired.

12. Sandwiches & Bread

Lunch was actually the hardest meal for me to figure out. Bread is often considered a poor choice that should be limited or even entirely removed on a low-histamine diet but sandwiches, bread, and muffins are such a go-to for most of us that it's hard (and isolating) to entirely eliminate them for long. Sandwiches are also tough because deli meats are a no for low histamine diets.

As I keep saying, this book is about a realistic approach to an OAS/low histamine diet. Some items (like yeast) are minimized instead of totally eliminated. Bread is a staple around the world and this selection of recipes shows that. It goes beyond what most of us think in terms of "bread", especially when used in the same sentence as sandwich. In addition, you can make your own bread with oat or rye flour if wheat is problematic for you. The biggest potential issue with bread is yeast but small amounts may be tolerated. After all my reading, and understanding that this is still a new field with a lot of unknowns, my personal opinion is that most bread isn't a big problem.

Generally speaking, "quick breads" rely more on baking powder than yeast and are more compliant, even in box mixes, so look for quick bread recipes. These are simple to make and easily altered to match your food needs.

Bread sometimes needs to rise in a warm space (particularly breads that need yeast), which can be tough inside. If you run into this issue and your house doesn't have anywhere particularly warm, set your oven to "warm." Allow it to heat up for five minutes before turning it off. Let the dough rest in the warm oven. Make sure you don't heat the oven so much that you heat or melt the container the dough is in or kill the yeast cultures. The goal is to simulate a warm summer window, not to bake the dough.

SkinnyTaste.com has an "easy bagel recipe" that has options for making them gluten-free, dairy-free, or egg-free, if you have a yen for fresh bagels.

Apple Cheese Melts

4 slices 1" thick-sliced tolerated bread

Set oven to broil. Put bread on ungreased cookie sheet. Broil with tops 4" from heat until golden brown, about 2-3 minutes.

¼ c. applesauce

4 oz. mild cheddar cheese

4 oz. goat cheese, crumbled

Optional Ingredients (add as your diet allows):

1 apple cut into rings

Remove bread from oven and flip. Spread with applesauce, apple rings (if tolerated), then cheddar and goat cheese. Broil just until cheese begins to melt, about one minute. Alternatively, toast the bread and add toppings, then broil 1-2 minutes.

Banana Bread

I also make banana quick bread from a nice, simple box mix.

2 eggs

2⅓ c. overripe bananas

Preheat oven to 350°F. Grease a 9x5 loaf pan. Beat the eggs. Mash the bananas.

2 c. flour

1 tsp. baking soda

¼ tsp. salt

Combine flour, baking soda, and salt.

½ c. butter

¾ c. brown sugar

In a separate bowl, cream butter and brown sugar. Stir in eggs and bananas until well blended. Combine all ingredients in one bowl and stir until just moistened. Pour into loaf pan and bake 60-65 minutes. Cool in pan for 10 minutes.

Beer Bread

You can use any carbonated beverage in beer bread. That means you can use soda or sparkling water. This is a nice way to enjoy a bit of some flavors you might be missing in life, like soda or beer.

3 c. flour, sifted*

*If you use self-rising flour, skip the baking powder and salt.

3 tsp. baking powder

1 tsp. salt

¼ c. sugar

12 oz. (1 can) beer or soda

¼ to ½ c. melted butter

Preheat oven to 375°F. Combine all ingredients except butter. For a softer crust, mix the butter into the batter too. Grease a loaf pan and pour the mixture in. For a crunchy, buttery crust, pour butter over the batter. Bake for 1 hour, then cool at least 15 minutes before eating.

Biscuits

By themselves, these are fairly bland. They are best served with gravy, or jam/jelly, or broken up in chicken soup like dumplings.

2 c. all-purpose flour

2½ tsp. baking powder

½ tsp. baking soda

1 Tbsp. sugar

SANDWICHES & BREAD

1 dash salt

Preheat oven to 400°F. Mix dry ingredients.

½ c. butter

¾ c. buttermilk (dehydrated is available)

Cut in butter so the mixture forms coarse crumbs. Add buttermilk. Knead on a lightly floured surface for about 2 minutes. Move dough onto an ungreased cookie sheet, form into a 6"x6" square and cut into 12 pieces. You can either leave the pieces connected or separate them and shape them like biscuits. Bake 15 minutes. Serve hot.

Cloud Bread

When you are don't have regular bread handy but do have eggs, this is one way to make a sandwich. If it ends up with something fairly runny after combining everything (like my first attempt), you can cook it for about 5 minutes less, just know that the final product will be flat like a crepe.

3 eggs

Separate eggs.

3 Tbsp. cream cheese

1 Tbsp. honey

Preheat oven to 350°F. Mix egg yolks, cream cheese, and honey until smooth.

¼ tsp. baking powder (or cream of tartar)

Combine egg whites and baking powder/cream of tartar in a glass bowl and whip egg whites until stiff peaks form. Gently combine all ingredients, being gentle so the egg whites don't completely collapse. Spoon 10-12 rounds on a greased cookie sheet. You can sprinkle rosemary or a tolerated spice on top. Bake 17-20 minutes on the middle rack, then move to broil for 1 minute, being careful not to burn them.

112

French Bread

When you write a cookbook, you get to include your favorites, and I really love a nice fresh loaf of French bread.

2¼ c. warm water

1 Tbsp. sugar

1 Tbsp. instant or active dry yeast

Combine water, yeast, and sugar. If you use active dry yeast, let it set until it starts to foam. This isn't necessary with instant yeast.

¾ tsp. salt

2 Tbsp. oil (canola, olive, vegetable, or avocado)

5½ c. all purpose or bread flour

Add salt, oil, and 3 c. flour and knead by hand for 2-3 minutes, or use a stand mixer with a dough hook. Add remaining flour ½ c. at a time. Dough should be sturdy, soft, and smooth, not sticky. Move into a greased bowl and cover with a towel or greased cling wrap. Put in a warm spot and let rise for an hour or so, until doubled in size.

Put dough on a floured surface. Divide in half. Pat or roll each section into a rectangle about 9"x13", then roll it into a cylinder, pressing out air bubbles as you go. Turn both ends in and pinch the seams closed. Round edges and put on a parchment sheet on a baking sheet, seam side down. If desired, make three diagonal cuts across the top of each loaf. (If you do it after it rises the second time and your knife isn't sharp enough, it could deflate the bread.) Let both loaves rise again until nearly doubled in size and puffy, about 1 hour.

After dough has risen two times (once in the bowl, a second time after being formed into a loaf), preheat oven to 375°F. Before baking, brush top with melted butter, if desired. Bake one loaf at a time on the center rack for 25-30 minutes. Tops should be golden-brown.

Original Source: MelsKitchenCafe.com (Easy Homemade French Bread)

Grilled Cheese (Gourmet)

Of course you can always make a regular grilled cheese with American cheese on a griddle, but this slightly fancier version is a nice change of pace and simple to adapt to your favorite/tolerated cheeses. It's surprisingly fast and easy to make, and you can even walk away while it cooks. (As a pet owner, I appreciate that.)

1 Tbsp. cream cheese

1 Tbsp. goat cheese

½ c. mild cheddar cheese

¼ tsp. garlic salt

Preheat oven to 450°F. Combine filling ingredients.

2 slices bread

2 Tbsp. olive oil

Baste outside of each slice of bread with olive oil and spoon filling onto inside. Bake 5 minutes, flip, and cook another 5 minutes.

Monte Cristo Sandwich

This is easy to change to suit your diet, such as by replacing non-compliant ham and Swiss with turkey and cheddar.

4 slices sandwich bread

4 slices Swiss cheese

2 slices deli turkey

2 slices deli ham

Stack a slice of bread, a slice of cheese, a slice of turkey folded in half, a slice of ham folded in half, a slice of cheese, and slice of bread.

1 Tbsp. butter

Heat a nonstick skillet over medium heat and melt butter in it.

2 beaten eggs

2 tsp. milk

Combine. Dip sandwiches in the egg mixture. Cook French toast style until golden brown, about 3-4 minutes per side.

You can also dip the sandwich in warmed strawberry or raspberry preserves or fruit spread.

Naan

I love nice fluffy naan but it often comes with garlic, herbs, or something else on top that I'm not sure I can eat. It's actually surprisingly easy to make, it just takes a little time since it has to rise.

2 c. flour

3 tsp. sugar

1 tsp. fast-rising yeast

Mix dry ingredients.

¾ c. water

2 Tbsp. olive oil

3 Tbsp. yogurt (Greek yogurt works)

Mix moist ingredients separately. Combine in one bowl until the dough just sticks together. Flour your hands and form it into a ball, then flour the outside of the ball. Grease the inside of a bowl large enough to allow the dough ball to double in size. Put the dough in the bowl and cover with cling wrap or a damp kitchen towel, then put it in a warm place to rise. In approximately ninety minutes, it should have doubled in size and be ready to cook.

Heat a non-stick skillet or iron frying pan on medium-high. Put dough on a floured rolling board and roll into a rectangle. Cut the rectangle into six equal pieces, which you will roll into six balls. Flour each of the six dough balls and put them to the side. Roll one out into a roughly circular shape. Turn the heat down to medium and put the first dough in the skillet. In 2-3 minutes, you should see bubbles on top of the naan. More bubbles generally equals more well-cooked. When you are satisfied with the number of bubbles, flip it over and cook another 2-3 minutes. Remove and cook the next one.

You can brush olive oil or butter on top before you flip it. You can also add garlic, rosemary, or another herb to the top.

Panini

This is more of a suggestion than a recipe per se. Panini's are basically hot, grilled sandwiches with both meat and cheese. They often have spicy mayonnaise, vinaigrette, or another tasty topping, as well as lettuce, tomato, and other standard sandwich toppings. Use what you can and enjoy! Panini presses make this fast and easy.

    Bread
    Meat
    Cheese

Build your sandwich. Grill it on both sides.

Sloppy Joes

I used to grab a can of sloppy joe mix or a packet of seasoning to make this. After my allergies made this impossible, I was excited to find an simple, tasty recipe.

    1 onion
    1 Tbsp. oil

Dice onion into small cubes. Cook over heat until soft, about 15 minutes. Add salt and pepper, if desired.

    1 lb. ground beef
    2 c. hash browns

Add ground beef and cook on medium until browned. Add hash browns and cook 5 more minutes.

    1 c. ketchup and 1 Tbsp. tomato paste OR 1 c. stewed tomatoes*
    1 Tbsp. Worcestershire or steak sauce
    *If you use mashed up hash brown patties, increase ketchup/stewed tomatoes to 2 c.

Add to beef mixture and cover. Simmer on low 20-25 minutes. Serve on buns.

Original Source: *Dad's Book of Awesome Recipes*

Stuffing (Matzo)

Stuffing is yummy but full of potential allergens. This version is actually not loaded with allergens, especially if you make your own matzo. It's also simple to customize by adding your own favorite (tolerated) veggies and spices, and even add-ins like bacon (if tolerated).

> Olive oil
>
> 1 carrot
>
> 1 apple

Dice carrot and apple. Preheat the oven to 375°F. Break matzos into pieces. Sauté carrots and apples in olive oil until they are soft, about 10-12 minutes.

> 1 12-14 oz. box matzo
>
> Pinch garlic powder
>
> Salt and pepper to taste

Add matzo and toast it for 2 minutes before adding any spices or personal favorite add-ins.

> 4 c. broth (chicken, turkey, vegetable, etc.)*
>
> 2 eggs, lightly beaten
>
> 2 sticks butter
>
> *Chapter 13 has a recipe for homemade chicken broth.

Grease a 9x13 dish. Dump matzo mixture into a large bowl and add the broth and eggs, then melted butter. Put mixture in the dish. Bake uncovered 45 minutes or until browned.

Original Source: JustaPinch.com (Matzo Stuffing)

Tortillas (Corn)

> 2½ c. corn flour (masa harina)
>
> ½ c. vegetable shortening
>
> 1 tsp. salt
>
> 1¼ c. water

Mix all ingredients until smooth. It shouldn't stick to your hands or flake apart. If it flakes, add water ½ tsp. at a time. If it sticks, add flour ½ tsp. at a time. Make 2" balls of dough and flatten them into a thin circle. Larger or smaller balls will result in larger or smaller finished tortillas. Cook on a dry griddle or frying pan with oil.

Zucchini Bread

My two year old was no more willing to eat vegetables than any other, but he loved his Aunt Blue's zucchini bread so much that she mailed frozen loaves halfway across the continent to him.

> 3 eggs
> 1½ c. sugar
> 1 c. vegetable oil
> 1 tsp. vanilla

Preheat oven to 350°F. Combine eggs, sugar, oil, and vanilla.

> 3 c. flour
> 1 tsp. salt
> 1 tsp. baking soda
> 1 tsp. ginger
> 1 tsp. baking powder

Optional Ingredients (add as your diet allows):

> 1 tsp. cinnamon
> 1 tsp. cloves

Add dry ingredients and mix.

> 2 c. grated zucchini

Add zucchini. Put in a greased loaf pan. Bake 45-60 minutes. Allow to cool 10 minutes, then remove from pan and cool on wire rack. Slice and enjoy when thoroughly cooled. Stores well frozen.

Original Source: Aunt Blue

13. SOUP

Watching the leaves falling and the temperature dropping may have impacted my choice to dedicate a chapter to soup, the ultimate cold weather comfort food. Even bland-sounding soups are warm and filling.

Soup is also the best comfort food when we are sick and those on a low histamine diet get sick too, we just don't have many options for ready-made sick-people food. Chicken soup, in particular, can be made in advance and frozen for sick days.

Just a reminder: **Fully cooking all ingredients is really important if you have OAS.** Butternut squash, carrots, and other vegetables in these soups can cause OAS symptoms if they aren't fully and completely cooked. Slow cookers are an outstanding way to both make soup and to ensure fruits and veggies are very well cooked, just remember that cooking won't stop some foods, particularly celery and spices, from causing reactions.

Comparison: Broth, Stock, and Bouillon

For professional chefs, the differences are important. For purposes of this cookbook, I use them interchangeably when I cook (based on what I have that is allergen-free) and you can too. True broth and stock have slightly different ingredients and cook times. Stock uses added bones but no added spices. Broth is made with meat but not necessarily bones, and usually has added spices and aromatics including garlic, carrots, and onion. Broth isn't cooked for as many hours as stock. Because it has fewer ingredients, stock may be better for people with allergies. Of course, boxed broth and stock in the grocery store can be fairly indistinguishable.

Bouillon cubes are a dehydrated, concentrated paste preserved with salt, making them incredibly high in salt, but they can be handy. I use them for soup when I have a hard time finding spice-free broth or stock. Bouillon is also very cheap and long-lasting, making it easy to keep on hand. You can make your own broth, stock, and even bouillon to suit your diet.

Butternut Squash Soup

This is one of my fall favorites and I know I'm not alone in that.

1-1½ lbs. butternut squash
1 Tbsp. butter (unsalted)
3 c. chicken broth

Peel, seed, and cut butternut squash into 1" chunks. Melt butter in a pot large enough to hold all ingredients. Mix in squash and broth. Simmer until squash is fully cooked and tender/ready to fall apart. It should take about 20 minutes. Puree chunks of squash in a blender.

Optional Ingredients (add as your diet allows):

Pepper, nutmeg, ginger, or cinnamon to taste

Return to pot and add optional spices.

Peanut Butternut Squash Soup

It may be clear at this point, but I really like peanut butter. I don't add peanut butter to everything, but it's a good source of protein and I need every bit of extra nutrients I can get.

4 Tbsp. peanut powder OR 2 Tbsp. peanut butter

Mix into butternut squash soup.

Carrot Soup

Carrots are a potential OAS issue, so don't eat this during the elimination phase. Without spices or toppings, this is super bland.

1 lb. chopped carrots

1 Tbsp. vegetable oil

2 c. vegetable broth

1-2 c. water

Optional Ingredients (add as your diet allows):

1½ tsp. ground curry or ginger

Combine vegetable oil and carrots in saucepan, coating carrots with vegetable oil. Add vegetable broth and bring to a low boil. Reduce heat and simmer until carrots are soft. Puree until smooth in a blender. Pour back into saucepan. If you want it thinner, add up to 2 c. water, depending on your taste. Heat until warm enough to eat.

Chicken Broth

There are more recipes online. It's really simple to make.

1 lb. chicken parts

6 c. water

Garlic to taste

Onion to taste

Optional Ingredients (add as your diet allows):

1 parsnip

Put all ingredients in a large pot. Bring to a boil, then lower heat. Cover and simmer for 1 hour. Remove chicken parts. Skim fat from the surface*, then strain stock through cheesecloth to remove larger particles.

*The matzo ball soup recipe in this chapter uses skimmed fat, so don't discard it if you plan to make that soon.

Chicken Noodle Soup

I have always loved a good cup of noodle soup, but my allergies mean I can no longer enjoy pre-packaged ones, so I'm including one.

¼ c. parsnips

1 c. carrots

½ c. onions

12 oz. egg noodles

Cook any vegetables thoroughly so you don't react to them.

4 c. cream of chicken soup (next page) OR chicken broth

1½ lb. chicken

Heat cream of chicken soup or chicken broth. Add remaining ingredients and simmer 10 minutes.

Original Source: MarthaStewart.com (Simple Chicken Noodle Soup)

Chicken Soup

This is exhibit one in why cookbook writers have to make every single recipe. This was a recipe for chili but the final result was soupy.

Having a minimal background in all things cooking, I used butter beans since they are, in fact, pretty much white, and that could be the reason it didn't turn out like chili. (It turns out that navy, Great Northern, cannellini, and baby lima are the standard "white beans.") It's even better if you make biscuits and break them up in the soup.

15 oz. (1 can) white beans, drained

Mash beans.

1 lb. boneless, skinless chicken thighs

4 c. chicken broth

15 oz. (1 can) white beans, drained (2 cans total in the recipe)

1½ tsp. salt

¼ tsp. pepper

½ onion, diced

3 cloves minced garlic

Optional Ingredients (add as your diet allows):

1 tsp. oregano

1 tsp. chili powder

1 tsp. ground cumin

Combine ingredients in a 3.5 quart slow cooker. Cook on high for 3-4 hours or on low for 6-8 hours.

1 c. corn

About 30 minutes before it's finished, stir in corn and re-cover.

Original Source: AmandasCookin.com (Crockpot White Chicken Chili)

Cream of Chicken or Turkey Soup

This is really just fancy, high calorie broth. It is definitely best viewed as the base for something else, in place of broth, unless you have someone sick who really can't eat much more than broth.

There's an old story "stone soup" where people keep adding little bits of this and that to "stone soup" (water with a stone in it). At the end, they are amazed how good the "stone soup" is because they don't realize they added all the ingredients for a "real" stew to the stone soup. This is kind of like that: add whatever you have on hand and enjoy, just make very, very sure it's cooked thoroughly and not old enough to cause histamine issues. By itself, this will be better than a stone in water but still as bland and unexciting as a bowl of broth.

½ quart chicken or turkey broth
½ c. heavy cream OR ½ c. half and half
⅛ tsp. salt
⅛ tsp. pepper

Bring the broth to a simmer. Slowly add cream. Add seasoning. Cover and let rest on lowest for 10 minutes. Serve it hot or cold but this is really best served as the base for something else, in place of broth. As your health improves, add cooked meat, peas, carrots, or potatoes and whatever spices you can tolerate.

Original Source: theSpruceEats.com (Cream of Chicken or Turkey Soup)

Hot and Sour Soup

This used to be one of my favorite things to order when we eat out. Since I can't have garlic, I added Chinese mustard powder for some heat. It isn't quite the same but everyone has their own favorite twists on recipes.

> 8 oz. mushrooms, preferably shiitake or baby bella
>
> 8 oz. (1 can) bamboo shoots

Slice mushrooms thinly and discard stems. Drain bamboo shoots.

> 8 c. chicken or vegetable stock (¼ c. set aside)
>
> ¼ c. rice vinegar, to taste
>
> ¼ c. soy sauce

Optional Ingredients (add as your diet allows):

> 2 tsp. ground ginger
>
> 1 tsp. chili garlic sauce OR 1-2 tsp. Chinese mustard powder

Put ¼ c. of stock aside. Combine ingredients and heat over medium-high until soup begins to simmer.

> 2 large eggs
>
> 8 oz. firm tofu

While soup heats, whisk eggs. Cut tofu into bite size squares.

> ¼ c. cornstarch
>
> ¼ c. chicken or vegetable stock

Combine set-aside stock and cornstarch until smooth. Stir into the simmering mixture.

> 4 green onions (scallions)
>
> 1 tsp. toasted sesame oil
>
> Salt and pepper to taste

Continue stirring while soup thickens, about 1 minute. Continue stirring as you drizzle in a thin stream of whisked eggs to create egg ribbons. Stir in tofu, half the onions, and sesame oil. Season with salt and pepper. Garnish with onions. Extra rice wine vinegar makes it more sour, extra chili garlic sauce or mustard powder makes it spicier.

Original Source: GimmeSomeOven.com (Hot and Sour Soup)

Lentil Stew over Couscous

When I made this, I had several quarts of leftover chicken broth from making matzo ball soup (with an incorrect recipe), 2 tomatoes, and a few other random vegetables. I used chicken broth instead of vegetable broth and tossed in all the random vegetables I had. It turned out fine, but it was just about the blandest meal in this book. I recommend adding spices.

> 3 c. dried lentils (1 lb.)
> 3 c. water
> 14 oz. (1 can) vegetable broth
> 14 oz. (1 can) diced tomatoes
> 1 large onion
> 1 green bell pepper
> 1 medium carrot
> 2 cloves chopped garlic
> 1 tsp. dried marjoram
> ¼ tsp. pepper

Combine in a slow cooker. Cover and cook on low until vegetables are tender, 8-9 hours.

> 1 Tbsp. olive oil
> 1 Tbsp. apple cider vinegar with the mother
> 5 c. hot, cooked couscous

Stir in oil and vinegar. Serve over couscous or other small pasta.

Original Source: *Allergy Free Cookbook*

Matzo Ball Soup

The original recipe called for 3-4 quarts of broth or salted water. The result was far too liquid. I'm sure they meant cups not quarts.

> ¾ c. matzo meal
> ¼ tsp. salt
> ¼ tsp. garlic powder

¼ tsp. onion powder

¼ tsp. pepper

Combine.

2 large eggs

2½ Tbsp. rendered chicken fat, grapeseed oil, or olive oil

In another bowl, mix eggs and oil/chicken fat. Pour into dry ingredients. Don't overmix. Let rest in the refrigerator for 45 minutes.

4 c. broth OR salted water

Start making 1" balls with the chilled matzo ball mixture while the broth or salted water comes to a boil over medium heat. Don't overwork the mixture. Lower to a simmer and gently lower the matzo balls into it. Cover and cook 30 minutes, until thoroughly cooked. Matzo balls absorb some of what they are cooked in. If you cook them in broth instead of water, they will taste like chicken (or vegetables) and be more flavorful, but it can be made either way.

For leftovers, remove the matzo balls and bring them to room temperature so they don't get mushy. If you will eat it soon, put both parts in the fridge in separate containers. If it will be more than a day or two, freeze it.

Original Source: ToriAvey.com (Sinker Matzo Balls)

Oatmeal Soup

There's no denying this is bland but it is warm, filling, and compliant. It's much better than I expected.

⅓ c. finely chopped onion

¼ c. shredded carrots

1 Tbsp. butter

½ c. quick or old fashioned oatmeal, cooked

Cook onion and carrots in 1 Tbsp. of butter over medium-low heat, stirring often, until both are thoroughly cooked. Cook oatmeal.

½ Tbsp. butter

¼ c. quick or old fashioned oatmeal, uncooked

3 c. chicken broth

Add remaining ingredients, including cooked oatmeal. Cook 3 minutes or until oats turn golden brown. Mix in broth and bring to a low boil. Add cooked oatmeal. Stir and bring temperature to medium. Cook 5 minutes.

Original Source: *The Quaker Oats Cookbook* (Quaker's Oatmeal Soup)

Peanut Soup

This is my favorite soup and a classic Virginia dish that dates bake to Colonial days. The first time I tried making it, the result was a total mess. I used peanuts and they just wouldn't chop finely enough to create a smooth texture. I have since read they should be soaked in water at room temperature 4 hours to overnight. The Washington Post had an online recipe that was very firm that your starting point must be peanuts, not peanut butter (much less powder!). However, I just don't have that kind of patience, so peanut powder it is for me.

1 Tbsp. unsalted butter

½ medium onion

Chop onion. Melt butter over medium heat. Add onions and cook 10 minutes, stirring often, until translucent and tender.

1 Tbsp. flour

3 c. chicken stock

Add flour and stir to coat onions, about 2 minutes. Slowly whisk in chicken stock and bring to a boil. Reduce temperature and simmer 20 minutes. Remove from heat and blend until smooth.

1½ c. peanut powder OR 1½ c. creamy peanut butter

½ c. heavy cream

Salt to taste

Over low heat, whisk in remaining ingredients for about 5 minutes. Don't boil! Finished soup should be smooth. Garnish with chopped peanuts or scallions, if desired. Serve warm.

14. Veggies & Side Dishes

We all know the drill: we need veggies to be healthy. Veggies are important to gut health and proper intestinal function, and eliminating large groups of food can mess with proper intestinal functioning. Oatmeal and adding flax seeds can help, but definitely don't just eliminate all veggies from your diet unless your allergist tells you to.

OAS makes fresh veggies difficult. Today, most of us have a ton of options available that go well beyond the carrots, peas, tomatoes, and other basics that are familiar and easy to grow in the yard. With literally an entire world of options, there are undoubtedly some that you can eat but it will take research and experimentation to figure out which ones those are, and that is best done after you finish the initial elimination phase and your body is in less of an uproar. Until then, your veggies need to be very thoroughly cooked but that doesn't have to mean flavorless. Despite the popular approach of drenching veggies in cheese, it also doesn't just mean "covered in cheese." Roasted vegetables are a quick, simple, healthy way to cook vegetables with little more than olive oil and a few herbs. Most of these recipes can easily be done with a variety of vegetables so experiment until you find something you love that loves you back.

Grains like quinoa and brown rice that aren't as heavily processed as white rice need to be rinsed before cooking to remove some excess starch. Quinoa and brown rice are both great sides. A simple meal of poultry with a side of either of these makes a great meal. Add some veggies and you have a reasonably balanced meal.

Baked Potato (Sweet or White)

These are the basis for quite a few other foods, and a tasty meal all by themselves. Cheese sauce and sour cream on potatoes are a classic.

Desired number of potatoes

Preheat oven to 350°F. Use a fork to make holes several places around the potatoes. If you want them to have a crispy skin, coat them in olive oil or butter. Bake 50-60 minutes, until very soft. (Larger potatoes may require more baking time.) If you are in a hurry, cut the potatoes in half and cook them on a baking sheet, skin side up for half the time, or stick a metal shishkabob skewer through the potato to help heat reach the center more quickly.

OR

Wrap each potato in cling wrap, being sure to cover the entire potato. Use a fork to make 6-10 holes around each potato. If you are out of cling wrap, remove a 1" deep sliver ⅛" wide running from one end to the other. Microwave smaller spuds for 5 minutes. Larger potatoes should be flipped and cooked another 5 minutes.

Corn Pudding

This makes a very large batch of corn pudding, highly appropriate for a pot luck or large family gathering.

4 c. (3 cans (15.25 oz.)) corn

1 Tbsp. cornstarch

1 tsp. salt

4 Tbsp. melted butter

1 c. milk

Preheat oven to 350°F. Combine ingredients.

3 eggs

Separate eggs. Beat egg yolks and add to mixture. Beat egg whites and fold in with other ingredients. Place in greased 9x12 casserole pan. Cook for 35 minutes. It's ready when it's firm.

Flax Fried Rice

Fried rice with some extra crunch from the flaxseeds. Yum! The first time I made this, when I went to stir the flax seeds on the burner, they started popping like popcorn!! This is a good way to use up small amounts of leftover meat, veggies, and rice. If you roast and crush extra flax seeds, you can add them to other meals for some extra taste and fiber in your diet.

¼ c. flaxseeds, crushed and roasted

Dry roast flax seeds over medium for three minutes, remembering to stir them. Crush seeds with a mortar and pestle.

1 c. long-grain brown rice

2 Tbsp. olive oil

3 eggs

½ c. chicken, turkey, or lamb

¾ c. vegetables

Optional Ingredients (add as your diet allows):

½ tsp. sesame oil

As the rice cooks, dice the meat and chop the vegetables. Beat eggs. Roast vegetables in the oven or start cooking in one skillet over medium for 5-10 minutes before you begin heat the oil and eggs in a second skillet over medium. Stir eggs as you fry for 3-5 minutes or until half cooked. Stir rice in quickly, coating in egg mixture and breaking up lumps. Reduce heat to medium-low. Add meat and vegetables. Cook an additional 4 minutes. Add remaining ingredients and cook a final 3 minutes.

Original Source: *The Anti-Inflammation Diet*

Fried Rice

This is a great, flexible side. While these are the classic ingredients, you can switch them around based on what you have and like.

4 c. cooked rice, preferably day-old

Rice can be white or brown but should be chilled, not fresh.

1 small white onion

2 medium carrots

1 c. peas

2 Tbsp. olive oil

Chop onion and carrots into small pieces. Thaw frozen veggies. Pre-heat a wok or skillet to medium. Add olive oil. Fry onion, carrots, and peas until soft. Slide to the side.

3 eggs

3 cloves minced garlic

Whisk eggs. Cook eggs in the open space, scrambling with a spatula. When eggs are cooked, mix in vegetables and garlic. Cook 1 minute.

Optional Ingredients (add as your diet allows):

2-3 Tbsp. soy sauce

2 Tbsp. green onions (garnish)

Add rice and soy sauce. Mix well and heat thoroughly. Garnish with chopped green onions.

Green Beans

I know for many, this is so simple that a recipe seems silly, but this book is also about remembering there are a lot of options. There is nothing wrong with simple boiled veggies. There's also nothing wrong with coating your veggies in a nice cheese sauce, if that's what it takes to get ~~me~~ you to eat it.

4 c. water

2 tsp. dried oregano

Boil water and oregano in a large saucepan.

1 lb. green beans, trimmed

Reduce heat and add beans. Boil 5-7 minutes, until tender. If OAS is an issue, cook for 15 minutes.

½ tsp. sea salt

¼ tsp. pepper

Strain and add spices.

Honey-Ginger Carrots

These are my favorite side in this book because the honey makes them sweet and I can eat ginger. If you can't eat ginger or don't like it, substitute whatever spice you prefer.

1 lb. carrots

Cut carrots into small pieces. If you are using them in the Honey-Ginger Sushi recipe, cut them lengthwise. If not, across (in circles) is fine. Cover with water and boil until tender, a minimum of 10 minutes. Drain.

¼ c. butter

2½ tsp. honey

In a large skillet, melt butter and honey over low heat.

1 pinch ground ginger

Optional Ingredients (add as your diet allows):

1 Tbsp. lemon juice or to taste

Stir in ginger and lemon juice (diet permitting), then carrots. Simmer until heated through.

Mashed Maple Squash

I seriously love this recipe, simple as it is.

1 winter squash (acorn, butternut, etc.)

The squash needs to be cooked thoroughly and cool enough to handle before you start the rest of the prep. Cut squash in half, remove all the seeds, and put the cut side down on a microwavable baking dish. Add ¼ c. water, cover with cling wrap, and microwave on high for about 20 minutes. Once it's cool, scoop the squash out of the skin, or just peel the skin and remove it.

2 Tbsp. butter

Heat the butter in a skillet. It is ready when it foams, starts smelling nutty, and browns a bit.

¼ tsp. salt

Add squash and salt and continue cooking for 5-10 minutes.

2 Tbsp. maple syrup

When that is done, stir in the maple syrup until well mixed. Serve warm.

Original Source: Cookistry.com (Blue Plate Special)

Mashed Potatoes

I know this is basic, but some of us need recipes for basic items. They are a key ingredient for Shephard's pie and lot of other meals.

6 potatoes

Peeling the potatoes or not is up to your taste and how much of a problem they are for you. Cut potatoes into chunks. Put chunks in cold water and boil until soft, 20-25 minutes. Pierce with a fork to confirm they are soft all the way through (and thoroughly cooked) but not mushy. Drain water.

⅓ c. milk

Optional Ingredients (add as your diet allows):

4 Tbsp. butter

Salt and pepper to taste

Mix all ingredients with a mixer or potato masher until desired consistency. Serve hot.

Mozzarella Sticks

This is a recipe I included because I really love getting mozzarella sticks when we eat out but can't any more. These start with that perennial kid favorite, string cheese sticks. This version doesn't have any spices, although you can definitely add your own favorites.

12 sticks of string or other cheese

Cut cheese sticks in half, creating 24 small sticks. Put in a freezer until completely frozen. Preheat oven to 400°F. Line a cookie sheet or baking tray with aluminum foil, baking spray, or parchment paper to keep the cheese sticks from sticking.

2½ Tbsp. bread crumbs

1 Tbsp. grated parmesan cheese

Combine.

2 Tbsp. flour

1 egg

Beat egg. You need three small bowls, one for the flour, one for the egg, one for the bread crumbs mixed with the parmesan cheese. Coat each cheese stick with the flour, then egg, and finally the bread crumb/cheese mixture. Place them on a lined baking tray and bake for 4 minutes. If they aren't fully crisp, put them in for another 2 minutes but keep a close eye on them so they don't melt completely.

Quinoa

This is a great substitute for rice and is healthy to boot. I was a hesitant to try quinoa because I had no idea what it was or how to make it but it's actually as simple as rice, and people have successfully made rice for thousands of years, long before timers or electric ovens. Quinoa comes in white, red, and black varieties. White is recommended as the best to start with.

1 c. quinoa

Before cooking quinoa, rinse it thoroughly by swishing under cool running water in a mesh strainer. This removes a natural coating that can make it taste slightly soapy or bitter.

1 tsp. olive oil

Heat over medium heat in a small saucepan. When it is shimmering, add quinoa. Cook about 2 minutes, stirring constantly, until quinoa is toasted.

1¾ c. water or broth

Add liquid (water or broth) and bring to a rolling boil. Reduce heat to lowest setting and cover. Cook for 15 minutes. Remove from heat and let stand for 5 minutes before removing the cover. If any liquid remains at the bottom, return to low heat and cook (covered) for another 5 minutes. Fluff and eat.

Rice, Brown

1 c. brown rice

6 c. cold water

1½ tsp. salt

Rinse brown rice in cold water for 30 seconds. Boil water and salt. Add rice and cook on medium-high for thirty minutes, stirring occasionally. Partially cover the pot. If you cover the pot completely it will boil over. Drain water off but keep rice in the pot. Cover tightly and let set for 20 minutes while steam finishes cooking the rice. Uncover, fluff, and eat.

Rice, White

My friends are sometimes surprised to see me making rice on the stovetop with no problems. I never understand their surprise because it really is as simple as this recipe. Double, triple, or quadruple this recipe, based on your family needs.

1 c. white rice

2 c. water

Boil water. Add rice. Simmer covered on low for 20 minutes. Remove from heat. My mother-in-law was adamant that the crispy rice on the bottom of the pan is a treat, especially for kids.

Roasted Chickpeas

Snacking is the easiest time for me to get into allergy trouble. I'll grab something small without reading all the ingredients, and wham! Roasted chickpeas make a good, simple snack to keep on hand.

3 c. (2 cans) canned chickpeas

3 Tbsp. olive oil

1 Tbsp. lemon juice

1 Tbsp. brown sugar

Optional Ingredients (add as your diet allows):

3 tsp. cumin

½ tsp. cinnamon

½ tsp. ginger

2 tsp. garam masala

¼ tsp. pepper

Pinch salt

Preheat oven to 400°F. Rinse and drain canned chickpeas. Add remaining ingredients. Spread on a baking sheet. Roast 30 minutes, stirring after 15 minutes.

Original Source: Scouting Magazine (Roasted Spicy Chickpeas)

Roasted Herbed Squash

1½ lbs. acorn squash, peeled and cubed (2" cubes)

2½-3 lbs. butternut squash, peeled and cubed (2" cubes)

1½ Tbsp. olive oil

1 Tbsp. minced rosemary

2 tsp. salt

½ tsp. pepper

Optional Ingredients (add as your diet allows):

1 Tbsp. minced thyme

Preheat oven to 425°F. Line a 15x10 pan with aluminum foil. Mix squash, oil, and seasonings and put in the pan. Roast for 20 minutes. Stir contents and cook an additional 20 minutes. If you have OAS, cook for an additional 20 minutes beyond that for a total of 1 hour. Broil 3-4" from the heat for 2-4 minutes for a darker color. Cool slightly.

5-6 oz. fresh goat cheese

2 tsp. warm maple syrup

Crumble the goat cheese. Add to squash and toss gently. Drizzle with maple syrup.

Original Source: TasteofHome.com (Roasted Herbed Squash with Goat Cheese)

Roasted Veggies

I wish I could say I love this, but I still not a veggie lover. I do, however, like this, and that's no small thing given how veggie-averse I have always been.

1 Tbsp. olive oil

3 red peppers

3 carrots

3 potatoes

3 parsnips

3 onions

1 can water chestnuts

1 sprig rosemary

Salt and pepper to taste

Preheat oven to 500°F. Pour oil in a roasting pan. Add vegetables and rosemary. Sprinkle with additional olive oil and toss so everything is lightly coated with oil. Roast 30-45 minutes, turning every 10 minutes, until everything is soft enough to easily cut with a spoon. Remove and throw away rosemary. Put what you don't eat immediately in a bowl, cover with olive oil, seal the bowl or cover it in cling wrap, and put it in the refrigerator.

Rosemary Roasted Potatoes

Potatoes (other than sweet potatoes) are potentially-problematic nightshades, but these are incredibly tasty.

1½ lbs. small red potatoes

1 tsp. crushed dried rosemary

2 Tbsp. olive oil

½ tsp. salt

Heat oven to 400°F. Cut potatoes in half and arrange in a shallow pan. Drizzle olive oil over potatoes, turning to coat all sides, then add rosemary and salt. Bake uncovered for 30-35 minutes, stirring occasionally until potatoes are tender when pierced with a fork.

Seaweed Salad

I put off making this for a long time because the original recipe was for seaweed soup. It didn't sound appetizing to me, either. However, with most salads off the table with OAS, this is an option.

1 oz. dried seaweed (~25 grams, or one package)

Break seaweed into bite size pieces and soak it in cold water for 10 minutes to rehydrate.

4-6 oz. water chestnuts*

1 Tbsp. olive oil

*One 8 oz. can of water chestnuts has a "dry weight" of 5 oz.

While seaweed is rehydrating, sauté water chestnuts in olive oil for 7-8 minutes. Drain water from the seaweed.

6 c. water

½ tsp. ginger or grated fresh ginger

Salt to taste

Add water and ginger (if desired) to the chestnuts and bring to a boil. Lower heat and simmer 20 minutes. Add salt to taste.

4 eggs

Whisk eggs, add to the mixture, and cook for an additional 3 minutes, until eggs set.

Optional Ingredients (add as your diet allows):

2 Tbsp. soy sauce

Drain off the excess water, add soy sauce (if tolerated), and it's ready to eat.

Tempura Vegetables

I've always been terrible about eating my vegetables but even I enjoy tempura vegetables. Panko is Japanese bread crumbs, which are lighter and airier than western versions. They also absorb less oil. Use any vegetables you like or have on hand. The ones in the recipe are just ideas. This makes A LOT of tempura batter, so you might want to cut it in half and drink half the can of seltzer water.

This also works great for shrimp tempura, but shrimp are a histamine issue so I'm not including that. If you want to make shrimp tempura, JustOneCookbook.com has a very helpful post on "How to Prepare Shrimp for Shrimp Tempura & Ebi Fry."

> 1 medium sweet potato
> ½ medium cauliflower crown
> ½ medium broccoli crown
> 1 medium onion

Slice sweet potato into ¼" strips and onion into thin strips. Break cauliflower and broccoli into small florets.

> 1½ c. tempura (or flour—rice, all-purpose, wheat, any kind)
> ½ tsp. salt
> 12 oz. (1 can) seltzer water or club soda, chilled

Whisk flour, salt, and seltzer together.

> 1-1½ c. canola oil

Pour half a cup of oil into a non-stick or cast iron skillet over medium-high heat. While the oil heats, coat veggies lightly in batter. You can hand-dip them or toss them using a flat whisk, which also allows extra batter to drain off. (I used a dipping fork designed for coating things with chocolate.) Put veggies in hot oil until crispy and very lightly browned on the bottom, 2-3 minutes, then flip and cook another 2-3 minutes. Don't crowd the pan. Remove and put on a paper towel to drain excess oil.

Before putting in the next batch of veggies, check oil and add up to an additional half cup. Allow oil to heat back up to near 360°F.

Seasoning options:

Sprinkle salt on the finished veggies as soon as you put them on the paper towels.

Add 1-2 Tbsp. of your preferred spices to the batter, as long as they are light enough to stay suspended in batter and cooking oil.

Original Source: ConnoisseurusVeg.com (Easy Tempura Vegetables)

TheKitchn.com (How to Make Tempura Fried Vegetables)

Twice-Baked Sweet Potatoes

These are a super-simple option for lunch, and easy to customize to suit your tastes.

> 1 medium sweet potato
> 1 oz. (2 Tbsp.) cream cheese OR young goat cheese

Optional Ingredients (add as your diet allows):

> 2 tsp. brown sugar
> ⅛ tsp. cinnamon

Preheat oven to 375°F. Poke 4-6 holes in potato that is scrubbed clean and bake until tender, 45-60 minutes. To bake in a microwave, wrap the potato in cling wrap, poke 4-6 holes in it and bake 5 minutes. Cool slightly.

Cut a slice from the top, enough to allow you to scoop out the pulp, leaving ¼" thickness on the outside. Mix pulp and remaining ingredients with fork and stuff the potato with it. Return potato to the oven and cook for another 15-20 minutes or 2-3 minutes in the microwave, until thoroughly cooked.

Original Source: TasteofHome.com (Creamy Twice Baked Sweet Potatoes)

15. SUSHI

The basic sushi recipe is two kinds of vegetables plus one source of fish. Both uncooked vegetables and fish (cooked or raw) can cause problems, which makes it hard to buy sushi and remain compliant with a low-histamine diet. Neither nori (seaweed) nor rice (brown or white) are histamine or OAS issues, so the real problem is compliant fillings. If you truly have a craving for sushi, you can technically wrap just about any food with rice and seaweed and make sushi. Take any food from this cookbook, use the "basic sushi" recipe, and you can have low-histamine sushi. Mix and match to create your own favorites! "MakeSushi.com" is a great place to learn about making sushi and for inspiration.

Sushi is also a great way to enjoy small amounts of problematic foods, when your body can handle it. It's also an *outstanding* way to use leftovers quickly. While you clearly want to eat food when it's as fresh as possible, sushi from leftovers makes a lovely lunch.

There is a ton of information online about making sushi but the two ingredients you simply must have are seaweed (nori) and rice. "Sushi rice" is preferable because its stickiness helps everything hold together, but it isn't a deal breaker. (Sushi rice is a specific kind of rice, just like brown rice and long grain rice.) If you enjoy sushi and can't find sushi rice locally, it's worth ordering it online.

While vinegar is on firmly on the "no" list for a low histamine diet, vinegar slows the growth of bacteria in the sushi, as it does for most food. Given the incredibly tiny amount you ingest in sushi, the benefit probably outweighs the risk. For more details, read "Inhibiting Bacteria Growth in Sushi" on ScienceNordic.com. That article also discusses how fresh wasabi can help slow bacteria growth.

If you use cream cheese, I think it's better from a block because a block allows you to cut it into slices. A tub really doesn't. I like adding it for the soft texture more than the flavor.

NOTE: Full cooking/assembly instructions are only given for the first recipe, "basic sushi". Refer back to this until you are comfortable with the basic techniques. The remaining recipes focus on the filling.

Sushi Rice

It is worth getting sushi rice to make sushi. It just is.

1 c. sushi rice (a.k.a., sweet rice or glutinous rice)

1 Tbsp. vinegar, preferably rice wine

3 c. water

Rinse rice repeatedly until the water remains clear. Boil water. Add rice and simmer uncovered for 10 minutes. Cover and simmer 10 more minutes or until all water has been absorbed. Remove from heat and cool for 10 minutes. Move rice to a bowl that isn't metal and add rice wine vinegar a little at a time. (Metal bowls may react to vinegar, giving rice a slight metallic taste.) Vinegar helps keep the grains of rice more separate, less mushy.

Not-Sushi-Rice for Sushi

White rice isn't strictly on either "no" list but brown rice is generally better for you. One end result of this diet is a potentially increased need for roughage and fiber, which is a need brown rice fills more effectively than white rice. Having tried sushi rice and not-sushi-rice, the sushi rice really is *much* better for sushi. But if it isn't available, it isn't available.

1½ c. short-grain rice or 1 c. long-grain rice

2 c. water (optional: add 2 Tbsp. extra water for stickiness)

Soak rice for 30 minutes to 4 hours. Boil water. Add rice and simmer uncovered for 10 minutes. Cover and simmer 10 more minutes or until all water has been absorbed. Remove from heat and cool for at least ten minutes.

Making Not-Sushi-Rice Stickier

Rice needs to be at least moderately sticky to help a sushi roll stay together. Sushi rice is naturally this way but other kinds of rice need all the help they can get to make them stickier.

- Short-grain rice tends to have more starch, and therefore be stickier, than medium- or long-grain rice. Jasmine and basmati are both medium-grain rice.
- Unlike sushi rice, don't rinse other kinds of rice repeatedly before cooking.
- Soaking non-sushi rice in water for 30 minutes to four hours before cooking may help make it be stickier.
- Letting cooked rice set in the pot longer can help it get stickier.

Basic Sushi Preparation

This is a short, probably over-simplified version of how to make sushi. Look online for videos if you need more help. As you practice and make more, you will learn your own family's preferences, just like with any other food. As I have made more sushi, I find myself using less and less rice. I now use about ¼ c. of rice per roll.

1 c. rice
1 sheet of nori (seaweed)
¾ c. filling

Put a sheet of nori shiny side down on the sushi mat*, spread rice from the top of the nori to the bottom and left to right, **leaving 2.5" on one side without rice**. Rice should be in a thin layer or the roll will end up far too thick. Put filling in a line from the top to the bottom near the edge with rice. You can put condiments such as wasabi in with the filling, if tolerated, or sprinkle in some spices.

*Rolling sushi is easiest with a sushi mat. They are inexpen-
sive and widely available, including online and in gift sets.
In a pinch, use a kitchen tea towel or a thick paper towel.

Moisten the end with exposed nori just enough so to be sticky.
The ends are normally dampened with rice vinegar but water can be
used. Fold the end near the filling over the filling, then roll the whole
thing up tightly until only the edge with exposed nori is left, being
sure to press the filling into the rice as you roll it. Roll over the
dampened nori and hold it tightly while it seals closed. Cut your sushi
into pieces with a sharp knife and serve. Make additional rolls if filling ingredients allow. Roll, cut, and eat.

Vinegar is on the low histamine "no" list but may be tolerated in
small amounts. As always, pay attention to how your body reacts.

Chicken Sushi

1 c. rice

1 sheet of nori (seaweed)

½ c. baked chicken

¼ c. roasted veggies

Spread rice on the nori. Make a line down the nori with chicken,
then with veggies. Roll, cut, eat.

Egg Sushi

1 c. rice

1 sheet of nori (seaweed)

¾ c. scrambled egg, omelet, etc.

Spread rice on the nori. Put egg in a line down the nori. Roll,
cut, and eat.

Fried Chicken Sushi

1 c. rice

1 sheet of nori (seaweed)

½ c. fried chicken or chicken tempura*

2 oz. cream cheese from a block (not tub)

*Tempura is a Japanese style of battering and frying.

Spread rice on the nori. Make a line down the nori with chicken, then slices of cream cheese. Roll, cut, eat.

Green Beans and Ham Sushi

1 c. rice

1 sheet of nori (seaweed)

½ c. ham

¼ c. green beans

Spread rice on the nori. Make a line down the nori with the ham and green beans. Roll, cut, eat.

Honey-Ginger Sushi

1 c. rice

1 sheet of nori (seaweed)

1 full carrot

½ c. baked chicken breast

2 oz. cream cheese from a block (not tub)

Spread rice on the nori. Cook carrot following the Honey-Ginger Carrots recipe, being sure to slice carrots into strips lengthwise instead of across (circles). Cut chicken into strips length-wise. Put pieces of each in a line from the top of the nori to the bottom starting about ¾ of the way down and add cream cheese beside it. Roll, cut, and eat.

Omelet Sushi

1 c. rice

1 sheet of nori (seaweed)

1 egg omelet with tolerated cheese

Optional Ingredients (add as your diet allows):

¼ c. roasted red peppers

Spread rice on the nori. Slice omelet into strips. Put omelet and optional red peppers in a strip down the nori. Roll, cut, and eat.

Philadelphia(ish) Sushi

Avocado is used in Philadelphia rolls but isn't compliant.

1 c. rice

1 sheet of nori (seaweed)

1 c. mixed roasted vegetables

¼ c. cream cheese from a block (not tub)

Spread rice on the nori. Put vegetables and cream cheese in a line down the nori. Roll, cut, and eat.

Pulled Chicken Sushi

1 c. rice

1 sheet of nori (seaweed)

¾ c. pulled chicken

Spread rice on the nori. Put chicken in a line down the nori. Roll, cut, and eat.

Roasted Squash Sushi

1 c. rice

1 sheet of nori (seaweed)

¾ c. roasted squash

¼ c. cream cheese from a block (not tub)

Spread rice on the nori. Put cream cheese and vegetables in a line down the nori. Roll, cut, and eat.

Roasted Vegetable Sushi

1 c. rice

1 sheet of nori (seaweed)

¾ c. mixed roasted vegetables

Spread rice on the nori. Put these in a line down the nori. Roll, cut, and eat.

Shepherd's Pie Sushi

1 c. mashed potatoes

1 sheet of nori (seaweed)

¼ c. green beans, fully cooked

½ c. lamb or chicken

1 carrot, fully cooked

Spread mashed potatoes on the nori. If desired, add any spice or herb you can tolerate to the vegetables and/or lamb. Slice carrots and meat lengthwise. Put green beans, carrot slices and lamb in a line from the top to the bottom of the nori. Roll, cut, and eat.

Thanksgiving Sushi

1 c. baked sweet or white potato

1 sheet of nori (seaweed)

½ c. baked turkey

2 Tbsp. cranberry sauce

Spread mashed sweet or white potatoes on the nori. Slice the turkey into strips length-wise. Spoon the cranberry sauce out in a line from the top of the sheet to the bottom. Finish by adding pieces of turkey, then roll, cut, and eat.

16. MAIN DISHES

I t seems like dinner would be hard, but it wasn't nearly as hard as lunch. In addition to a variety of ways to make chicken, there are a lot of casseroles that can be simplified enough to be compliant.

In general, histamine is produced as food ages and proteins break down. That means you should eat your all food as soon as possible after buying it and that meat, being mostly protein, has the potential to create problems more quickly than other foods. It also means that you should opt for whole pieces over pre-ground or pre-sliced. More surface area=faster histamine accumulation.

Beef and shellfish are off the table for now, but poultry (chicken and turkey) and lamb are good. Many of these dishes specify chicken but turkey or lamb can be used too. Cured meats including bacon, salami, pepperoni, and hot dogs are high-histamine and, sadly, not compliant. They also tend to have ton of other ingredients (and spices) mixed in, which just adds to the potential problems.

CCC Casserole

My son came home from Scout camp raving about this. We tried an oven-made version and really enjoyed it. When my allergies got worse, I experimented to find a chili-alternative that works. Delish!

> ½ lb. ground chicken, turkey, or lamb

Brown the ground meat.

> 1 can (14 oz.) chili OR 1 can kidney beans+10 oz. stewed
>   tomatoes

Drain excess grease and add chili. Mix and stir until it reaches a boil, then simmer for about five minutes.

1½ c. crushed corn chips

1 c. cheese, grated

Put the corn chips in the bottom of a 9x9 baking dish. Add the meat and chili mix, then top with cheese. Cover and bake at 350°F for 20 minutes.

Original Source: Boy Scout Campouts

Cheesy Black Bean Burgers

15½ oz. (1 can) black beans

1 lb. ground chicken or turkey

1 egg

1 c. shredded mild cheddar cheese

⅓ c. plain bread crumbs

½ tsp. garlic powder

Preheat the grill to medium. Drain and rinse the black beans, then mash until smooth but a bit chunky. Add remaining ingredients. Shape into 8 patties, 16 if you prefer sliders. Grill until fully cooked, about 4 minutes per side, depending on meat used.

Original Source: *The Moms' Guide to Meal Makeovers*

Chicken and Cheese Quesadilla

Quesadillas can be changed in a virtually infinite variety of ways. This is a simple one to start with. Once you are comfortable with this, experiment with fillings you enjoy.

½ c. cooked chicken or turkey breast, shredded

½ c. cheese, such as mild cheddar or a taco cheese mix, shredded if possible

2 corn tortillas

Heat a non-stick or cast iron skillet on medium-high. When it's hot, reduce to medium. Place chicken and cheese to taste on a tortilla, fold it in half, then put it on the skillet. In a few minutes, the cheese will start melting and the bottom will be browning. Flip each tortilla and finish cooking. Remove from heat and eat.

If your health allows, you can add salsa, preferably without tomatoes, but should refrain from sour cream. ("Soured" items aren't compliant with a low histamine diet.) For a different taste, try adding chutney.

Chicken Breast

This is great to add to pasta, sushi, and other meals.

Chicken or turkey breast

2 oz. olive oil

Herbs of choice (rosemary, oregano) or salt and pepper

Heat a skillet and coat with 1 oz. olive oil. Coat the chicken breasts with olive oil and herbs, or salt and pepper. Cook over medium for about 10 minutes, until the edges are cooked, then flip. Cover and cook 10 more minutes.

Chicken Strips

Chicken strips are also great with Shake and Bake mix (page 66).

1-2 eggs

Preheat oven to 450°F. Break eggs into a bowl. Lightly beat with a fork.

Salt and pepper to taste

¼ tsp. garlic powder

1 bag plain potato chips (4 oz. or more)

Crush chips and combine with spices in a sealable container.

4 boneless, skinless chicken breasts

¾ c. flour

Cut chicken into strips and dust with flour. Dip into eggs. Coat with chips. Lay chicken strips on a greased baking sheet. Bake 18-20 minutes, flipping halfway through, until golden brown and crispy.

Chicken Teriyaki

> 1 c. chicken broth
>
> ½ c. teriyaki sauce
>
> 3 garlic cloves, minced

Optional Ingredients:

> ⅓ c. brown sugar

Combine.

> 1 lb. chicken, diced

Add chicken to mixture. Pour mix into slow cooker and cook on low for 4-6 hours.

Chicken Vegetable Medley

I've made this since high school. It's another great way to use bits and pieces of leftover vegetables and meat. It's also a great way to get the family to try new things by including little bits of them.

> 2 chicken or turkey breasts
>
> 1 can watercress

Optional Ingredients (add as your diet allows):

> 4 medium potatoes or parsnips
>
> 3 medium carrots
>
> 3 peppers

Slice chicken, carrots, peppers, and potatoes into bite size pieces. Put in a 10" skillet with watercress. You can use any vegetables you can tolerate but be sure they are thoroughly cooked.

> ½ c. water

Add water to skillet and heat to a boil. Reduce heat. Cover and simmer 15 minutes.

> 10 oz. green peas

Rinse peas under cold water to separate. Add and cook until fully heated. Serve.

Gyoza

Gyoza needs some vegetables in the filling. Swap out anything you can't eat for something you can. They are best steamed or fried.

> 1 pkg. gyoza wrappers (no real need to thaw them)
>
> ¼ lb. chicken or turkey*
>
> 1 can water chestnuts
>
> 1 Tbsp. olive oil
>
> 1 tsp. ginger powder
>
> Permitted vegetables to taste
>
> *Leftover taco meat makes a great start to gyoza filling since it's already seasoned.

Optional Ingredients (add as your diet allows):

> ½ c. carrots
>
> ½ c. peppers
>
> 2 Tbsp. mushrooms

Grate carrots. Mince the other solid ingredients into small pieces. Mix everything together. Gyoza wrappers can be frozen when you start filling them. Use your finger to moisten one edge of the wrapper so it stays shut when crimped. Spoon 1 Tbsp. filling into the center of each wrapper, fold wrapper in half, and crimp the edges shut so nothing falls out. Continue until you are out of wrappers or filling.

Put finished gyoza in a non-stick or greased skillet or wok over medium heat with 2 Tbsp. of water. Cover and steam for 5 minutes. Remove lid and continue cooking for 5 minutes, then flip them. Cook 5 more minutes. Check to be sure they are fully cooked before serving. If not, flip and cook 5 more minutes. You can freeze leftovers to eat later.

You can also fry gyoza.

Gyoza sauce is half vinegar and half soy sauce, mixed, and isn't compliant.

Honey-Apricot (or Peach) Chicken

> 4 fresh apricots OR 2 peaches (1 can of either, in a pinch)

Pit fruit and cut into wedges.

> 2 chicken breasts
> ½ tsp. salt
> ½ tsp. pepper

Cut chicken into bite size pieces. Sprinkle chicken with salt and pepper, if tolerated. Heat oil over medium-high and brown chicken on both sides, 3-5 minutes per side.

> 3 cloves minced garlic
> 2 Tbsp. honey

Reduce heat to medium-low and add garlic, honey, and fruit. Cover and simmer until meat and fruit are all thoroughly cooked. If desired, uses the roasted apricot or peach recipe in chapter 8.

Original Source: AllRecipes Magazine June/July 2018 (Honey-Apricot Pork Chops)

Lamb Chops with Rosemary and Garlic

I'm not a huge fan of lamb, but these were really good and lamb is very compliant. Of course, I had to make it without the garlic.

> 6 cloves garlic
> 1 tsp. salt

Mince garlic with salt.

> 2 Tbsp. dried rosemary
> 2 Tbsp. olive oil
> ½ tsp. pepper

Add to garlic/salt mixture.

> 12 lamb chops, bone-in and frenched*
> *This is part of the butchering process. Just ask the butcher at your grocer to make sure they chops are frenched.

Rub both sides of chops with the mixture. Wrap in foil and re-frigerate 30 minutes to 3 hours. Grill or broil over medium high for 2-5 minutes per side. When finished, it will be rosy pink near the bone when you cut a slit to check.

Macaroni and Cheese

It's a well-loved comfort food, but this version is healthy. You can't even taste the squash.

> 3 c. dry pasta

Prepare pasta according to instructions on the box.

> 1 Tbsp. olive oil
> ½ c. roughly chopped white onion
> 2 cloves garlic, minced

While pasta boils, put olive oil in a large pot over medium heat. Cook onion and garlic thoroughly, about 5 minutes.

> 1½ c. vegetable broth
> 3 c. diced butternut squash, about ¾ of a medium squash
> ¼ tsp. each salt and pepper

Add broth, butternut, salt, and pepper to onion/garlic mixture. Simmer 7-10 minutes, until butternut is thoroughly cooked. Puree until smooth.

> 1 c. shredded mild cheddar cheese
> ½ c. plain Greek yogurt

Strain the pasta and return to pot. Add puree and cheddar cheese. When that is well mixed, add yogurt and stir until well mixed.

Original Source: AmandasCookin.com (Butternut Squash Mac and Cheese)

Meatballs

These are great with pasta or fried rice, or in a meatball sub.

> 1 lb. ground chicken or turkey
> ¼ c. milk

½ c. bread crumbs

¼ c. grated cheese

1 egg

1 tsp. salt

Mix all ingredients. Form into 1-2" meatballs. Larger meatballs will take longer to cook.

1-2 Tbsp. olive oil

Heat a frying pan on medium heat and coat with olive oil. Add meatballs and cook covered (to retain moisture) until light brown on all sides, 15-25 minutes, depending on the size of the meatballs. You can add meatballs to pasta or roasted veggies, or make a meatball sub/sandwich.

Original Source: *The Kid's Cookbook: Yum! I Eat It*

Meatloaf

I sought out a meatloaf recipe because my husband likes it and it seemed like a good comfort recipe to include. To my surprise, I loved it and so did my parents!

1 lb. ground chicken, turkey, or lamb

2 cloves roasted, finely diced garlic

1 egg

30 round buttery crackers (approximately 1 sleeve)

¼ tsp. salt

Optional Ingredients (add as your diet allows):

¼ tsp. ground pepper

¼ tsp. thyme

Preheat oven to 350°F. Smash crackers to crumbs with a mortar and pestle. Combine all ingredients in a bowl and mix well by hand, without kneading it, until just combined. If it feels too soggy or loose, add more crumbled crackers. Put into a lightly buttered loaf pan and bake about 50 minutes. Finished meatloaf needs to be 160°F in the center, as measured by a meat thermometer. Remove from the oven and let rest for 10 minutes before slicing.

If this has too much carbs for you, you can make it with as few as 10 crackers.

Original Source: Cookistry.com (Blue Plate Special)

Muffin Pizzas

Since I can't eat garlic, pre-made pizza is out for me and I don't always want a full-size pizza. This is my solution.

6 English muffins, cut in half

8 oz. pizza sauce, stewed tomatoes, or similar

Grated cheese

Toppings as tolerated

Preheat oven to 350°F. Slice muffins in half. Put approximately 2 Tbsp. of sauce on each half. Add cheese and toppings to taste. Bake 15-20 minutes.

Parmesan Panko Pork Chops

Panko is a lighter, crispier version of bread crumbs. It can be used for all kinds of meat and fish, as well as tempura, and (like tempura) can also be used for vegetables.

1 c. panko bread crumbs

⅓ c. grated Parmesan cheese

Preheat oven to 375°F. Lightly oil a baking sheet. Mix Parmesan and panko.

Salt and pepper to taste

6 center cut pork chops cut ¾" thick

Salt and pepper the pork chops.

½ c. flour

Egg wash (1 egg+1 Tbsp. water whisked together)

Dredge pork chops in flour, then egg wash, then panko crumbs.

Olive oil

Place chops on the baking sheet and drizzle the tops with olive oil. Bake 35 minutes, flipping after 15-20 minutes. Chops are done when internal temperature reaches 145°F. Let rest 5 minutes before serving.

Original Source: RockRecipes.com (Baked Parmesan Panko Pork Chops)

Parmesan Wings

This is another recipe I made for my husband that he really enjoyed. It would make a great appetizer for a tailgate party or just about any kind of potluck.

½ c. breadcrumbs

⅓ c. grated parmesan cheese

1 tsp. garlic powder

Preheat oven to 325°F. Combine.

12 chicken wings

½ stick butter, melted

Dip wings in butter, then mixture of other ingredients. Put in 9x12 casserole dish. Bake 45 hour. Flip and cook 15 more minutes.

Original Source: *Cooking with 4 Ingredients*

Pasta with Cream Cheese

If your kids are just learning to cook, this is a great place to start because it's so simple. For variety, you can replace plain cream cheese with flavored cream cheese, such as garlic and herb.

2 c. uncooked bowtie pasta

16 oz. mixed vegetables

Thoroughly cook pasta and vegetables. Drain.

8 oz. cream cheese

Add cream cheese. Cook 1-2 minutes, stirring constantly. Cream cheese should be melted and coating everything.

Pasta with Peas

This is actually my favorite, or at least most-made, lunch in this cookbook because it's fast and easy, and it reheats well.

> 2 c. chicken or vegetable broth
>
> ½ c. water
>
> ¾ c. (6 oz.) couscous, pastini, or other small dried pasta
>
> 1½ c. frozen peas
>
> ¼ tsp. onion powder
>
> ¼ tsp. ground ginger or several slices fresh ginger (to taste)

Combine ingredients in a medium saucepan. Bring to a boil over high heat. Reduce heat and cook at a low boil for about 5 minutes, until pasta is tender. Don't drain.

> 3 eggs
>
> ⅓ c. grated Parmesan cheese

Beat the eggs. Add eggs and cheese to other ingredients and stir constantly as you cook 2-4 minutes, until the eggs are fully set. If there is excessive water, drain some off. As you add more food into your diet, you can add chunks of chicken, additional vegetables, and tolerated spices for variety. If you used fresh ginger, remove it before storing any leftovers to prevent it from overpowering everything else.

Original Source: *The Moms' Guide to Meal Makeovers*

Pita Pocket Pizza

You can pack the bread and small containers with sauce, etc. and assemble this when it's time to eat.

> Pita bread
>
> Tomato or other tolerated sauce
>
> Grated cheese
>
> Toppings (including other kinds of cheese or precooked chicken strips) as desired

Cut the pita pocket in half and fill with a spoonful of pizza sauce, a spoonful of cheese, and whatever else you enjoy. This is pizza, not science, so the amounts and toppings are based on what the eater enjoys. Bake over a camp fire, on a grill, or in the oven at 400°F for 5-10 minutes. Cool slightly before eating.

Pizza

I miss pizza. I seriously miss pizza, but I'm allergic to garlic. If you also miss pizza but have allergy issues, it's still possible to enjoy pizza. There are tons of recipes for pizza on the internet, in books, and lots of other places. The basic process is make (or buy) a crust then put sauce and toppings on it. Simple to say, less simple to do.

   1 crust

   1 c. sauce (barbeque, tomato, white, etc.)

   2 c. cheese

   Toppings to taste

Prepare crust first, then sauce. Pour sauce over the crust while the oven preheats, per instructions for the crust. (Pesto sauce may be too oily.) Sprinkle cheese over sauce. Add toppings. Cook.

I like to use leftovers on my pizza. A small chunk of cooked chicken (shredded) is enough for a pizza topping, but not for much more. I also love goat cheese on pizza. Parmesan cheese is particularly good with pesto sauce, which uses parmesan cheese in it. Most of the time, I use mild cheddar because I know I don't react to it.

Pulled Chicken

Despite my fears, this was quick, simple, and tasty. It is one of the most surprising (to me) successes I had in this cookbook.

   4 boneless skinless chicken breasts cut into thirds

   1 Tbsp. apple cider vinegar with the mother

   2 Tbsp. brown sugar

   ⅔ c. barbeque or other tolerated sauce*

   ¼ c. water

   *I tried this recipe with sweet and sour sauce (double recipe) but it came out a bit too soupy for a sandwich. If you use something other than barbeque sauce, add it slowly to prevent it becoming soupy.

Use a liner for your slow cooker. Combine ingredients in slow cooker. Cover and cook on low for five hours or on high for 2½ to 3 hours. Remove chicken with a straining spoon. Shred chicken with two forks. Return chicken to the pot and mix into the cooking liquid.

⅔ c. barbeque or other tolerated sauce*

Add additional sauce. Barbecue sauce is generally tomato-based and not well tolerated but pulled pork/chicken is yummy, so try to find a sauce you can tolerate or make the one in this book. Grocery stores now carry smaller slider buns in addition to regular size burger buns, if you prefer a smaller sandwich.

Shake and Bake Chicken Tenders

My tween said this "isn't as bad" as other kinds of homemade chicken. I'll take what I can get: he eats it.

Shake and Bake mix (page 66)
Chicken strips (or other protein)

Dump enough of mix to coat all the protein into a gallon zippered plastic bag. Rinse chicken or other protein. Pat dry. When excess water is gone, put protein in the bag, seal it, then shake to coat. Remove and put on a lined cookie sheet. Bake at 425°F for 15-20 minutes.

Original Source: TheBlackPeppercorn.com (Homemade Shake n Bake)

Shepherd's Pie

This filling, tasty treat is a favorite of my parents that I ate as a kid and recently rediscovered. I love that it's actually low histamine, especially if you swap out the white potatoes for sweet potatoes. It's also great because it actually calls for lamb, it isn't a substitute for another meat.

3 medium white or sweet potatoes OR equivalent in mashed potatoes

Peel and quarter the potatoes. Put them in a pot and cover with at least an inch of cold water and bring to a boil. Reduce and simmer until tender, about 20 minutes.

> ½ stick butter
>
> 1 c. each of 2-3 mixed vegetables, as tolerated (diced carrots, corn, peas, green beans, peppers, etc.)

You can use as little as 1 c. of one kind of vegetables, but it tastes better with closer to 3-4 c. total.

Melt butter in a skillet over medium heat and sauté vegetables, starting with carrots because they take longer. Peas and corn cook quickly so add them when other vegetables are almost fully cooked. Cook all problematic vegetables very thoroughly. Alternatively, use vegetables from one of the "side dish recipes" such as honey-ginger carrots or roasted peppers and skip the butter.

> 2 lbs. ground lamb

When vegetables are very nearly cooked, add lamb to the skillet and finish cooking the mixture.

> ½ c. broth
>
> Salt, pepper, and spices to taste

Add salt, pepper, and broth. When the broth starts simmering, reduce heat to low and cook uncovered for ten minutes. If the lamb starts drying out, add more broth. Preheat oven to 400°F. Mash potatoes. Spread lamb and vegetable mixture evenly in the bottom of a 9x9 casserole dish and top with mashed potatoes. Cook about 30 minutes, until browned and bubbling.

Original Source: SimplyRecipes.com (Easy Shepherd's Pie)

Shishkabobs

These are a summer classic and easily modified to fit your families allergies and tolerances, but most tend to rely on veggies that aren't easy to cook thoroughly enough to avoid OAS symptoms on a shishkabob skewer. When they are cooked enough, they tend to fall apart and fall off the skewers.

Ham and pineapple brushed with sweet and sour sauce is a classic combination.

    skewers

    1 lb. protein or meatballs

    ½ lb. sweet potatoes

    ½ lb. tolerated veggies

    ½ c. sauce

Cut all ingredients into bite-size pieces. Alternate ingredients on the skewers. Brush with a tolerated sauce. Cook over medium heat until thoroughly cooked, 6-8 minutes (more for OAS concerns). Use any tolerated vegetables, making sure they are thoroughly cooked.

Spiced Lentils

I had these at Scout leader training. My patrol had to find a filling meal that worked around my allergies and this is what they came up with. Of course, we skipped the garlic and onions. (Tomatoes are non-compliant for a low histamine diet, but I wasn't on that then.)

    1½ c. uncooked rice

Cook the rice. Preparing the rest of the meal should take approximately the same amount of time as making rice, so preparing them simultaneously works well.

    1 small yellow onion

    3 cloves garlic

    1 Tbsp. olive oil

Chop the onion and garlic. As the rice cooks, fry the onions and garlic in a splash of olive oil until soft.

    1 c. dry lentils (any color)

Add lentils and dry-cook for 2-3 minutes.

    3 c. water

Add 3 c. water and cook until absorbed, about 15 minutes.

14.5 oz. (1 can) tomatoes

Optional Ingredients (add as your diet allows):

Chicken or other meat, to taste

Spices to taste or ½ tsp. each: salt, coriander, turmeric, ginger

Add tomatoes and spices. Optional: add chunks of chicken or other meat. Simmer 15 minutes, then taste and add spices, to taste.

Original Source: OneIngredientChef.com (Dal Bhat Nepalese Lentil Curry)

Stuffed Acorn Squash

This is another meal I started making in college, then forgot about until I had to go searching out compliant meals. I love it!

1 lb. ground chicken, turkey, or lamb

½ c. chopped, peeled apple*

*The apples don't need to be thoroughly cooked before you stuff the squash, but they do need to be thoroughly cooked before you eat them. If apples aren't causing you a problem, you don't need to cook them before you stuff the squash.

Brown the meat. Add the apples.

2 medium acorn squash, seeded

Microwave squash for 5 minutes, then cut in half top to bottom.

4 c. cooked brown rice

Combine rice, meat, and apples. Stuff squash with mixture. Cover with cling wrap and microwave until squash is cooked through and soft, about 5 minutes.

½ c. shredded cheese

Top with the cheese and microwave 1 more minute.

Stuffed Chicken

The original recipe called for a full slice of cheese and 1-2 Tbsp. of pesto per breast. I have no idea how they managed to get that much into a chicken breast without slicing it in half. I was able to get closer to 1 tsp. of pesto sauce and ¼ to ½ slice of cheese per breast. This is a great recipe to experiment with. Try stuffing chicken with anything and everything you enjoy, including different sauces.

> Chicken breasts
>
> Pesto or other sauce
>
> Sliced cheese
>
> 2 oz. olive oil
>
> 1 Tbsp. butter

Cut a slit in the chicken breast. Stuff with sliced cheese and sauce. Heat a skillet and coat with 1 oz. olive oil. Coat chicken breasts with olive oil and herbs, or salt and pepper. Preheat oven to 350°F. Cook over medium for 4-5 minutes per side, then flip. Put 1 Tbsp. butter in a casserole dish. Put in preheated oven just long enough to melt butter. When chicken is done on the stovetop, put it in the casserole and bake an additional 25 minutes, covered.

Stuffed Shells

As a kid, this felt like a fancy restaurant meal but it's actually quite simple to make at home. It does take a little time, though.

> Approximately 18 large pasta shells

Preheat oven to 350°F. Prepare shells following package instructions.

> 24 oz. ricotta cheese
>
> 3 c. shredded mozzarella
>
> 2 eggs
>
> Pepper, herbs (as tolerated)

Optional Ingredients (add as your diet allows):

> ¼ c. grated parmesan cheese

Mix cheeses and eggs. If you can tolerate pepper and herbs, fold them in. Lightly coat a 9x12 pan with butter.

Olive oil

Lightly coat shells with olive oil and stuff with cheese mixture. Put them in the pan and cook 20 minutes.

As you expand what you are eating, you can switch one cup of mozzarella for 4 oz. young goat cheese and use white or tomato sauce (recipes in Chapter 8) instead of coating with olive oil.

Sweet Potato Gnocchi

These are incredibly tasty. We had them plain but some roasted veggies could have made them spectacular. They are also good frozen and reheated, which I love. If I make a nice big batch and freeze them, I have something to eat busy weeks or while I'm getting past a reaction.

1½ lbs. sweet potatoes

Bake potatoes. After removing and discarding skins, mash the rest thoroughly. Throw away stringy bits.

¼ c. sweet rice flour (mochiko or glutinous rice flour)*

1 Tbsp. lemon juice

1 tsp. salt

½ tsp. xanthan gum

½ tsp. pepper

*sweet rice flour is gluten-free, despite the name

Optional Ingredients (add as your diet allows):

½ tsp. nutmeg

Mix mashed sweet potato with remaining ingredients. Scoop portions of dough onto a floured work surface. Roll into ½ inch thick ropes, then cut into ¾ inch pieces, which you will form into ovals. Use the tines of a fork to make ridges on the ovals, then freeze them for at least 30 minutes before cooking.

1 Tbsp. olive oil

Heat olive oil in a skillet on medium. Cook gnocchi for 3-5 minutes per side, until lightly browned and warmed through, turning once. Add extra oil as needed to prevent sticking.

Original Source: *Allergy-Free Cookbook*

Turkey (Brined)

This needs to be started nearly a week in advance but it makes for an incredibly yummy turkey. It also looked spectacular when it came out of the oven on Thanksgiving.

14-16 lb. frozen turkey

Thaw in the refrigerator for 2-3 days before submerging in brine.

1 gallon vegetable stock

1 c. kosher salt

½ c. brown sugar

1 Tbsp. peppercorns

1½ tsp. chopped, candied ginger or grated fresh ginger

Optional Ingredients (add as your diet allows):

1½ tsp. allspice berries

Combine ingredients in a large stockpot over medium-high heat to create brine, stirring periodically until it boils. Make sure all solids dissolve. Cool to room temperature and refrigerate until 12-24 hours before you plan to eat. It needs to brine for 8-16 hours, depending on how much flavor you want to impart.

1 gallon heavily iced water

5 gallon bucket

Combine brine and ice water in the 5 gallon bucket. Remove the turkey innards and put the turkey in the brine, breast side down. Discard turkey innards unless you need them for another recipe. Weigh the turkey down to keep it fully immersed for the entire 8-16 hours it is stored in a cool place or refrigerated prior to cooking, if needed. Turn the turkey halfway through but ensure it remains fully immersed until you are ready to cook it.

Put the oven shelf on the lowest level and preheat to 500°F. Remove the turkey and dispose of the brine. Rinse the turkey inside and out with cold water. Put a roasting rack inside a half sheet pan and put the bird on it. Pat dry.

1 red apple, sliced

1 c. water

Optional Ingredients (add as your diet allows):

1 cinnamon stick

Microwave the apple, cinnamon (if tolerated), and water on high for five minutes.

4 sprigs rosemary

6 leaves sage

Canola oil

Add rosemary and sage and put it inside the turkey. Tuck the wings underneath and coat skin generously with oil. Roast turkey at 500°F for 30 minutes. Remove turkey and stick a probe thermometer into the thickest part of the breast. Reduce the temperate to 350°F and return it to the oven. In 2-2½ hours, it should be cooked to 161°F. (If the thermometer has an alarm, use it.) Loosely cover with foil and let rest for 15 minutes before carving. Use juices from the pan for gravy.

Original Source: FoodNetwork.com, courtesy of Alton Brown

Zoodles (zucchini noodles)

Zucchini

Use a spiralizer on zucchini to create spiral "noodles" to use in place of pasta.

17. SNACKS

Some of these are sweet, some are savory, but all are simple to make, store, and carry. A few (chocolate covered pretzels and cinnamon glazed almonds, in particular) make good gifts.

Tips for Melting/Dipping Chocolate

Several recipes call for melted chocolate. Here are some tips for melting chocolate and dipping things in it.

- If you search for "candy decorating tools" the results should include inexpensive tools (less than $10 for some sets) for dipping things in chocolate. There are different tools depending on the shape and relative weight of what you are dipping.
- "Dipping chocolate" may require extra steps (tempering) but have a better result than chocolate chips.
- Microwave on 50%, not full power, to reduce the chance of burning it.
- If most of it has melted, stir the chocolate chunks so the rest of the chocolate can melt it.
- Place chocolate dipped items on parchment or wax paper to prevent/reduce sticking.
- Don't store chocolate in the fridge for more than a few days.
- Try using the chocolate sauce recipe (Chapter 8).

Candied Nuts

This is a good snack. It's also a great gift, especially for Teacher Appreciation Week and Christmas.

2 c. unsalted nuts

Preheat oven to 400°F. Spread nuts evenly on a jelly pan or similar rimmed baking sheet. Toast until fragrant, stirring once, usually 6-8 minutes. Allow pan to cool and lien with parchment paper, or line a second pan with parchment paper if you are in a hurry.

¾ c. sugar

½ tsp. kosher salt

2 Tbsp. water

Combine sugar, salt, and water in a large skillet. Simmer until it turns amber colored, 12-15 minutes. SWIRL, do not stir, the simmering liquid. Stirring will crystallize the caramel. Add nuts. Line the cooled pan with parchment paper and spread the nut mix on top, separating nuts as much as possible. After it has cooled, break up any large clusters.

Cheez Crackers

If you leave the dough in the freezer too long, it will turn into an orange rock that needs to be thawed. Don't make an orange rock.

1 c. flour

4 Tbsp. cold butter, cut into small pieces (*not* melted)

8 oz. shredded mild cheddar cheese

¾ teaspoon of sea salt

Put ingredients in a food processor and pulse until mixture is crumbly.

4-5 Tbsp. cold water

Add cold water to the cheese crumble by the tablespoon and mix it until dough forms. Roll the dough into a ball and wrap it in cling wrap. Freeze the dough ball for at least 30 minutes to ensure it is cold the whole way through. The colder/harder your dough is, the easier it will be to handle, so don't take it out early, but don't leave it until it get rock solid.

Preheat oven to 350°F. Remove the dough from the freezer. Put it between two sheets of parchment or wax paper. Use a rolling pin to flatten dough until it's about ⅛" thick, then cut it into 1" squares with a pizza cutter or knife. Sprinkle with sea salt and bake 20-25 minutes. There is a fine line between golden and burnt with these so watch them carefully.

Chips (potato, zucchini, or other vegetable)

> Potato, zucchini, sweet potato
>
> 1 Tbsp. olive oil
>
> Sea salt or flavored salt to taste
>
> Pepper to taste

Preheat oven to 450°F. Cut vegetables into thin slices. A mandolin slicer works well for this. Toss with remaining ingredients.

Optional: Top with seasonings like ranch mix or garlic powder. Bake 25 to 30 minutes, flipping halfway through.

I tried this with cucumber, potatoes, and baby carrots. The carrots came out as charcoal but the cucumbers weren't even slightly crispy. The potatoes were just right but far better fresh from the oven than a day later. As they cooled, they lost crispness.

Chocolate Covered Pretzels

A nice, inexpensive set of chocolate dipping tools make these even easier and more fun. They are a great present and are super simple to decorate to suit the occasion by sprinkling toppings on them.

> Pretzels (rods are easiest)
>
> White chocolate (chips, bark, bars–any kind will do)
>
> Toppings (sprinkles, coconut, colored sugar, cookie crumbles, whatever your body can tolerate)

Line cookie sheet with wax paper. Melt chocolate in the top of a double boiler or in a microwave for 30 seconds at a time (to prevent burning) until melted or nearly melted, or use chocolate sauce (Chapter 9). Dip pretzels in chocolate. Shake or drip off excess and lay pretzels on the cookie sheet. While chocolate is still warm, scatter on toppings.

For a two-tone chocolate pattern, melt white, cherry, butterscotch or other chips in addition to the chocolate. Pour second color chocolate into a sandwich bag, snip the corner, and drizzle over the first layer. Chill or freeze until set. Store loosely covered in a cool, dry place. It also works with chips, although they get soggy quickly.

Cinnamon Glazed Almonds

Egg whites aren't low histamine and almonds are a clear allergen, but.... Every year, parents struggle to find a good, affordable present for teachers. Every year, I buy a 3 lb. bag of almonds at Costco™ and make cinnamon almonds for every single teacher my boys have. They love it–the boys *and* the teachers! So, even if your family can't eat these, they may have a place in your home, or your gift-bags.

⅓ c. butter, melted*

2 egg whites (room temp)

1 c. sugar

3 c. almonds

4 tsp. cinnamon

*For three pounds, you need exactly two sticks of butter.

Preheat oven to 325°F. Combine all ingredients except almonds. Mix in almonds. Pour onto a pan with raised edges, such as a jelly roll pan, to keep ingredients from dripping off the edges.

Bake 50 minutes, turning every 10 minutes, until almonds are crisp. It's easier to remove them from the pan when they are still warm. When cool, the butter/sugar/egg mixture gets very hard, making it harder to remove the nuts from the tray. It also makes it seem like a nightmare to clean, but hot water melts it like, well, butter.

Glazed Popcorn

This reminds me of popcorn coated in a hard candy like Jolly Ranchers™.

> ¼ c. butter
>
> 3 Tbsp. light corn syrup
>
> ½ c. sugar
>
> 1 pkg. (4-serving size) gelatin (any flavor)

Heat butter and syrup over low heat. Stir in sugar and gelatin, and bring to a boil. Preheat oven to at 300°F. Reduce stovetop heat and simmer mixture gently 5 minute.

> 8 c. (2 qt.) popped popcorn (plain)

Put popcorn in a bowl. Pour mixture over popcorn, tossing to coat well. It quickly cools and hardens, so try to have the popcorn ready when the glaze is done. Spread on greased or lined jelly roll or similar pan, or use parchment paper. Bake 10 minutes. Cool. Remove and break into small pieces.

Golden Fish Crackers

These don't look amazing but they are tasty. My family tells me that with chili powder, they do taste like real Goldfish Crackers™.

> 2 slices real American cheese (not "cheese food")

Preheat oven to 400°F. Stack the slices of American cheese and cut them into 16 squares. You do not need to remove the plastic because *real* American cheese doesn't come in individual, plastic-encased slices. Separate the 32 squares.

> ½ tsp. salt

Optional Ingredients (add as your diet allows):

> ½ tsp. powdered ginger
>
> ⅛ tsp. garlic powder
>
> ⅛ tsp. chili powder

Combine spices. Coat cheese squares with it. Arrange squares on a parchment paper lined baking sheet or silicone baking mat, leaving enough space between crackers to allow for cheese to melt. After 7-7½ minutes, they should puff up and be well-browned–almost, but not quite, burnt. They'll be soggy if they are undercooked. These are best enjoyed within a few days.

Original Source: KeyIngredient.com (Stella Style Goldfish Crackers)

GORP

This can be very compliant or far from it, depending on what you choose to add. For example, I love Craisins® but cranberries are less compliant than raisins.

> nuts
> cereal (Cheerios™, Chex™, etc.)
> Cheez-Its® or similar crackers
> Raisins
> M&Ms®
> white chocolate chips
> Other bite-size food you enjoy

Dump them in a bowl, mix them, bag 'em up, and go.

Granola Bar

I think these are such a great snack that I have different versions in each of my cookbooks.

> 2½ c. old fashioned oats
> ½ c. nuts, roughly chopped

Preheat oven to 350°F. Bake oats and nuts on a rimmed baking sheet until lightly toasted, 8-10 minutes.

> ¼ c. honey
> ¼ c. butter
> ⅓ c. brown sugar

While oats cook, heat honey, butter, and brown sugar over medium until sugar dissolves into melted butter. Remove from heat.

> 1 tsp. vanilla
>
> ¼ tsp. kosher salt
>
> ¾ c. mix-ins (¼ c. each of 3)

Stir into sugar mixture. Pour over oat/nut mixture, being sure to moisten all oats. Add mix-ins, except chocolate (if used). Line a 9"x9" baking dish with parchment or aluminum foil and lightly grease or spray with cooking spray. (You will use this parchment or foil to pull the bars out of the pan.) If using chocolate, wait until mixture is cool (about 15 minutes), then stir in chocolate. Place mixture in pan, pressing mixture flat. Chill for 2 hours, then cut and serve.

Original Source: BlessThisMessPlease.com (Granola Bar Recipe)

Marshmallows

I had no idea these could be homemade until I saw "homemade marshmallows" at the grocery store. They smell a bit like gym socks at one point in the process but they end up tasty.

> 3 envelopes gelatin (unflavored)
>
> ½ c. cold water

Sprinkle gelatin over cold water in a bowl. Soak 10 minutes.

> 2 c. sugar
>
> ⅔ c. corn syrup
>
> ¼ c. water

While gelatin is soaking, combine sugar, corn syrup, and water in a small sauce pan and bring to a hard boil for 1 minute. Pour the boiling mixture into gelatin water and mix at high speed.

> **Warning:** The mixture will "climb" the beaters so watch them and keep pushing it down to prevent a big mess.
>
> ¼ tsp. salt
>
> 1 Tbsp. vanilla
>
> Confectioners' sugar (for dredging)

Add salt and beat for 12 minutes. Add vanilla. Oil a piece of cling wrap and line a 9" x 9" pan with it before scraping the mixture into it. Press the mixture flat with a second piece of oiled cling wrap. Let set for several hours before removing and cutting into pieces with kitchen (food only) scissors. Dredge with confectioners' sugar.

Twix™-like Candy Bar

The website "TheSpruceEats.com" has a collection of tasty homemade candy bar recipes, like this one. Homemade at least allows you to control the additives and even decrease the sugar and other problematic ingredients.

1¼ stick butter, softened

½ c. sugar

Preheat oven to 350°F. Line a 13x9 casserole pan with parchment paper or aluminum foil and grease the foil or spray it with non-stick cooking spray. Mix butter and sugar until light and fluffy, about 3 minutes.

2 c. minus 4 Tbsp. flour

½ tsp. salt

Add flour and salt and mix on low until just combined. Press the shortbread mixture into a prepared pan, in a thin, even layer. Bake 18-20 minutes, turning halfway, until it is a light golden brown. If it overcooks, it will be crumbly. Allow to cool completely before continuing. If you use homemade caramel, start it when the shortbread finishes baking and it will be cool at the perfect time to add the caramel.

21 oz. caramels

2-3 Tbsp. heavy cream

If you use homemade caramel, follow the recipe below but after it simmers for 7 minutes, add heavy cream and simmer for 3 more minutes. Pour an even layer over cookie crust and freeze for 1 hour.

For store-bought caramel, combine with heavy cream and microwave until melted and smooth. Stir every 30 seconds. If it's too stiff, add additional cream 1 tsp. at a time. Pour over cookie crust in an even layer. Freeze for 1 hour to fully set the caramel.

1 lb. semisweet chocolate or chocolate flavored candy coating

Use the foil or parchment as handles to remove the caramel covered shortbread from the pan. The cookie base will probably crumble if you don't use a sharp knife when you cut them into finger-width bars, or whatever size you prefer.

Microwave the chocolate to melt it, stirring every 20-30 seconds. Dip frozen bars into the melted chocolate, covering them completely, before putting them onto a parchment or wax-paper-lined tray. When all the bars are done, refrigerate for 10 minutes to set the chocolate. They will remain good for about 1 week.

Original Source: TheSpruceEats.com (Make Your Own Twix Bars at Home) They have recipes for a lot of different candy bars.

18. DESSERTS

First, the bad news: Chocolate is a potential histamine problem, but white chocolate is generally well tolerated (depending on added ingredients). Sugar is generally bad too, so use moderation.

Now, the good news: There are lots of sweet treats you can enjoy, especially cookies, you just may need to bake. You can also look online for ways to substitute applesauce and/or honey for sugar to make your treats healthier and even more compliant.

Dessert has actually been the easiest for me by far because the hardest thing for me is avoiding spices, and desserts are generally light on spices. Cinnamon is the spice I encounter the most in desserts, although allspice, cardamom, nutmeg, and a few more are fairly common. Desserts are also light on uncooked fruits and vegetables, which is, of course, the main problem for OAS. Cookies, cakes, and desserts are almost the only area where I feel comfortable picking up something from a buffet and eating it. (I also eat some cheese and crackers at buffets.)

Berry Pie

After I made berry compote the first time, I pondered what to do with it other than adding it to yogurt or cottage cheese. Pie seemed like the thing to do, especially since it makes a fairly healthy, low-sugar pie.

Triple batch of berry compote (can be mixed berries)
1 refrigerated pie crust

3 Tbsp. corn starch

Prepare a triple batch of the berry compote with one or more kinds of berries (page 71) using ⅓ c. honey a 2 Tbsp. lemon juice. While the compote is simmering, put the pie crust in the pan and preheat the oven to 450°F. Add cornstarch to filling 1 Tbsp. at a time to thicken. Pour compote into the crust and bake 20 minutes. Let cool and firm 15-20 minutes before eating.

Blondies

One night, we came home to find our middle schooler proudly displaying the (remaining) half pan of blonde chocolate chip brownies (blondies) he had made, using a recipe from his middle school Family and Consumer Science class (FACS–modern Home Ec). Score one for public education!

⅓ c. butter, softened

1 c. firmly packed brown sugar

1 egg

1 tsp. vanilla

Preheat oven to 350°F. Mix butter and sugar. Add egg and vanilla.

1 c. flour

¼ tsp. baking soda

¼ tsp. salt

½ c. chocolate chips

In a separate bowl, combine flour, baking soda, and salt. Mix into butter mixture, then stir in chocolate chips. Pour mixture into a greased 8x8 pan. Make sure mixture is spread evenly. Bake 25-30 minutes. Cool for 10 minutes.

You can add hot fudge, butterscotch, or caramel (Chapter 9).

Brown Sugar Cookies

I love how simple and allergen-free these are.

¾ c. packed brown sugar

1 c. butter, softened

1 egg yolk

2 c. flour

Cream sugar and butter until light and fluffy. Add in egg yolk, then flour. Refrigerate for 1 hour. Preheat oven to 325°F. Form into 1" balls and put on lightly greased baking sheet. Flatten and crisscross with fork. Bake 12-14 minutes.

Chocolate Chip Peanut Butter Cookie Variation

Add the following ingredients to brown sugar cookies before refrigerating, then follow the rest of that recipe.

2 Tbsp. peanut powder + 1 Tbsp. water

¼ c. chocolate chips

Original Source: *Cooking with 4 Ingredients*

Cheesecake

I have long baked "Chantal's New York Cheesecake" from AllRecipes.com, but it uses sour cream, which is not compliant. Personally, I like cinnamon or chocolate graham crackers for the crust.

1½ c. crushed graham crackers*

½ c. white sugar

¼ c. butter, melted

*15 graham crackers is one short of two packages, and one box generally contains three packages.

Preheat oven to 400°F. Mix crushed graham crackers, sugar, and butter. Press into the bottom of a greased a 9" springform pan.

5 (8 oz.) packages cream cheese, softened

5 eggs

2 egg yolks

Mix until smooth.

1½ c. sugar

¼ c. heavy whipping cream

6 tsp. flour

Add to egg/cream cheese mixture and mix until it's smooth again. Pour onto the crust and bake at 400°F for 10 minutes. Turn the oven down to 200°F and bake for 1 hour or until filling is set. If it's still jiggly, cook it a little longer. The first time I tried this, I used an older oven and it took nearly 2½ hours to fully cook! Cool the cake in the closed oven, if possible, to reduce cracking. This may take several hours. Refrigerate.

As you feel better, add toppings. Berry compote makes a great cheesecake topping, as do caramel and chocolate sauce.

Original Source: AllRecipes.com (Cheesecake Supreme)

Chia Pudding (Blended)

Chia pudding can be enjoyed with whole seeds or blended. If you would prefer it as a drink, you can leave it set at room temperature for 10 minutes instead of refrigerating. This will allow the seeds to absorb the milk and plump up.

2 c. milk (coconut milk works)

½ tsp. vanilla

½ c. chia seeds

Whisk milk and vanilla together. Whisk in chia seeds and any desired mix-ins. Blend for 1-2 minutes, until smooth. Refrigerate at least 2 hours to fully set. It is best eaten within a few days.

Optional mix-ins:

Since it is really quite bland, this is a great recipe to personalize with seasonings (cardamom, cinnamon, extract flavorings) and add-ins (dried blueberries, granola) that you enjoy, as you are able.

¼ c. maple syrup

1 Tbsp. honey

½ c. fresh blueberries or blackberries

¼ c. granola

German Apple Cake

This recipe was a handout in my high school German class that I translated into English. My teacher never expected anyone to actually bake it, but this recipe makes one tasty apple cake.

4-5 apples

Peel apples and cut into slices.

1½ c. flour

2 tsp. baking powder

Mix the flour and baking powder.

¾ c. butter

½ c. sugar

1 tsp. vanilla

Combine the butter, sugar, and vanilla until creamy.

4 eggs

4 Tbsp. milk

Preheat oven to 400°F. Add eggs and milk to sugar mixture a little at a time, keeping the mixture creamy. Add flour mixture a little at a time until dough forms. Pour into a greased 9" Springform pan. Layer sliced apples on top. Bake 40 minutes.

1 Tbsp. butter

1½ Tbsp. sugar

Brush the top with butter and sprinkle with sugar. Allow cake to cool and firm before removing the outer ring from the pan.

Original Source: handout in high school German class (true story)

Gingerbread Cookies

A Christmas classic, my family enjoys eating gingerbread cookies year-round. This recipe has been approved by my tween. However, while dark molasses works well, don't use "blackstrap" molasses. I did this. Blackstrap is more concentrated and the cookies were not good. ((Shudder)) Not good AT ALL with blackstrap. Not a one of us could even finish a single cookie. Not. One. They all went into the trash.

  1 c. sugar

  1 c. light molasses (a.k.a., cane syrup)*

  1 c. (2 sticks) butter

Combine sugar, molasses, and butter in a sauce pan. Boil, then remove from heat.

  1 Tbsp. baking soda

  1 tsp. salt

Add baking soda and salt <u>but be prepared</u>: **it reacts**! Be prepared for it to double in size even before you add any other ingredients.

  2 eggs, beaten

  4¾ c. flour

Optional Ingredients (add as your diet allows):

  2 tsp. cinnamon

  2 tsp. ginger

  ¼ tsp. all spice

Stir in eggs. Mix in flour and tolerated spices. Chill dough. Roll and cut out cookies. Bake at 375°F for 5-7 minutes. Cool baked cookies for 30 minutes before decorating.

Graham Cracker Pie Crust

Making these at home reduces potential allergens, and it's easy. Personally, I strongly prefer using a mortar and pestle to crush the crackers rather than a plastic bag, which may get holes poked in it.

It's easy to make a cinnamon or chocolate flavored crust by using chocolate or cinnamon graham crackers. It isn't even an extra step or ingredient! Just remember to read all the ingredients on the cracker box.

1½ c. graham cracker crumbs

6 Tbsp. butter, melted

Optional Ingredients (add as your diet allows):

¼ c. sugar

For crust, crush the graham crackers thoroughly in a mortar and pestle or in aplastic bag with a rolling pin. Mix with sugar. Cut in butter and press into a 9" pie pan. Bake at 375°F for seven minutes. Remove and cool for ten minutes before filling.

Oatmeal Cookies

This looks like kind of a lot of ingredients but they are all basic, simple ingredients. Nothing unusual about them.

¾ c. butter

1 c. brown sugar

½ c. sugar

1 egg

¼ c. water

1 tsp. vanilla

1 c. flour

1 tsp. salt

½ tsp. baking soda

3 c. rolled oats

Preheat oven to 350°F. Mix ingredients in a bowl. Drop onto a greased cookie sheet by rounded spoonfuls. Bake 12-15 minutes.

Peanut Butter Fudge

In 3rd grade, our teachers decided to teach one recipe every month for the school year. This was one of them, and I still love it. So does everyone else who tries it and survives the massive sugar shock. (Note: **Diabetics should avoid this fudge at all costs!!**)

In the course of writing this and another cookbook, I discovered that these are basically the center of a buckeye chocolate!

1 lb. butter

1 lb. peanut butter

2 lbs. confectioners' sugar

Optional Ingredients (add as your diet allows):

4 Tbsp. cocoa powder

Melt the butter. Mix in peanut butter, then the sugar and cocoa powder. You can also swirl the cocoa powder in for a different effect. It melts *very* easily, so it's best to keep this fudge refrigerator.

Rice Pudding

This is one my teen and I enjoy making and eating together.

1½ c. cooked white rice

1½ c. milk

¼ tsp. salt

Combine rice, milk, and salt in a saucepan over medium heat, stirring until creamy and thick, which should be about 15-20 minutes.

½ c. milk

1 egg, beaten

⅓ c. white sugar

Add additional milk, egg, and sugar, continually stirring and cooking for 2-3 minutes or until egg is set.

1 Tbsp. butter

½ tsp. vanilla

Remove from heat and add the butter and vanilla. If you can tolerate cinnamon, it is good on top of rice pudding. Enjoy!

Original Source: AllRecipes.com

Shoofly Cake

This was my Grandma's recipe but my brother taught it to me. Originally, I'm sure it came from the Amish since they are the ones who make the far more famous shoofly pie.

2 c. sifted flour

1 c. sugar

½ c. shortening

Preheat oven to 350°F. Mix flour, sugar, and shortening into crumbs. Remove ½ c. crumbs.

½ c. warm water

½ c. molasses

1½ c. baking soda

Make a well in the crumb mixture. Pour in water and molasses. Add baking soda and mix until blended. Pour into an ungreased 9" square pan. Sprinkle reserved crumbs on top. Bake 35-45 minutes.

Shortbread Cookies

My husband has always managed to (tactfully) let me know when my culinary efforts don't quite hit the mark. This shortbread is one recipe he has loved since the very first time I made it, even going so far as to prefer it to the famous-maker brand in the store.

3 Tbsp. sugar

1¼ c. flour

½ c. butter (no substitutions)

Preheat oven to 325°F. Mix dry ingredients. Cut in butter until well mixed and fine crumbs form. Knead until smooth. Pat or roll dough into your desired shape but it shouldn't be more than ½" deep. You can press the dough into an ungreased pie pan or cookie sheet, or roll it flat and use cookie cutters. You can also bake it in silicone cookie molds. Before cooking, cut into the shape you want the final cookies. The baked cookies are too hard to cut without crumbling if you skip this step. If desired, use your fingers to scallop the edges. Bake 25-30 minutes. Finish cutting shapes, if needed, after removing from the oven. Cool 5 minutes before transferring to a wire rack to finish cooling.

As your diet allows, you may add spices like cloves, ginger, lemon peel, and poppy seed, or even sprinkles for special events.

OPTION: Caramel Shortbread

Make the caramel recipe while the shortbread bakes. When the shortbread comes out of the oven, pour caramel over it and cool in a refrigerator. Sprinkle with coarse sea salt, if you like salted caramel.

Original Source: BH&G Christmas Cookies magazine 1998

Snow Cream

This can be made with shaved ice or snow. If you use snow, put a clean bowl out to catch fresh snow. If you live in an area prone to smog or dirty air, wait until enough snow has fallen that it's clean before you start collecting snow to eat. You really don't want to eat dirty snow, so use shaved ice if you aren't sure or if it's not winter.

1 c. milk OR 1 can (14 oz.) condensed milk

1 tsp. vanilla

⅓ c. sugar

Combine all ingredients. If desired, add a few drops of flavored extract, sprinkles, or even cocoa powder.

8 c. clean snow OR shaved ice

Gradually add snow. If it's not thick enough, add more snow. Eat it before it melts!

Sugar Bombs (frozen Buttercream Frosting)

Kids like frosting. They often eat the frosting and toss the rest of the cake or cupcake. This goes directly to their love of frosting. It sounds insane, but one Sugar Bomb is actually less sugar and less mess than one cupcake.

½ c. solid vegetable shortening

½ c. butter

1 tsp. vanilla

Cream the butter and shortening with an electric mixer. Add vanilla.

4 c. (1 lb.) confectioner's sugar

Gradually add confectioner's sugar until everything is mixed, scraping to ensure everything on the bottom and sides is mixed in.

2 Tbsp. milk

Add milk to dry-seeming mix and beat until light and fluffy. Use white or add food coloring designed for frosting. It is ready to use as frosting.

For sugar bombs, fill silicone ice cube trays and freeze. Pop out one frozen "sugar bomb" at a time. They melt quickly, so eat them soon after removing them from the freezer.

Sugar Cookies

My kids always want the frosted sugar cookies at the grocery store. And, as a good mom, I feel obligated to try at least one to ensure they are safe. Making them at home is a no-brainer.

2¼ c. sifted flour

1 tsp. baking powder

1 tsp. salt

Mix dry ingredients in a small bowl and set aside.

¾ c. butter, softened

1 c. sugar

2 eggs

½ tsp. vanilla

Mix wet ingredients thoroughly in a separate bowl. Add dry ingredients. Chill 1 hour.

Preheat oven to 400°F. Place rounded spoonful onto ungreased baking sheet and sprinkle with optional sugar or sprinkles. Bake 6-8 minutes. Let cool and frost when cool, if desired.

Thousand Layer Cake

Also called Spekkoek or Lapis Legit, I read about this cake in the *Crazy Rich Asians* trilogy and was curious. Thousand Layer Cake is made by alternating plain and spiced layers of cake, baking each one for just a few minutes before adding the next. Truthfully, it takes too much time to make on an average night but for special occasions? The non-compliant ingredients are easily modified, and all the butter and eggs make it rich and indulgent.

$\frac{1}{2}$ lb. butter, softened

1 c. sugar

1 tsp. vanilla

Line the bottom of a Springform pan (approximately 9") with parchment paper and butter the sides. Cream butter and sugar, add vanilla.

10 large eggs, separated

Separate eggs. Put whites in a separate bowl. Add yolks to the butter mixture one or two at a time.

1 pinch salt

Mix egg whites and salt, and beat until stiff peaks form. (I recommend reading theSpruceEats.com post "All About Whipping Egg Whites" if you don't already know how.)

1 c. all-purpose flour, sifted

Fold egg whites into the yolk mixture and gently combine, then add sifted flour.

Flavoring for the Second Layer (add as your diet allows):

2 tsp. cinnamon

1 tsp. ginger

$\frac{1}{2}$ tsp. nutmeg

$\frac{1}{2}$ tsp. cardamom

$\frac{1}{4}$ tsp. clove

OR

1 Tbsp. flavored coffee creamer

OR

1 Tbsp. cocoa powder

Pour half the mixture back into the second bowl and add spices, cocoa, or flavored coffee creamer.

Preheat the grill/broiler to 350°F. Start with the baking rack on the highest rung and move it down as you bake, so the top of the cake cooks without burning. Depending on how many layers you want and how much time you have, alternate baking anywhere from 2 Tbsp. to ½ c. of the two batters. Tap the Springform pan gently on the counter to reduce bubbles before baking each layer.

Coat the bottom of the pan with the first layer of batter, then bake for about 3 minutes. Because each layer is so thin, they burn easily and must be checked frequently. Each layer should be firm and light brown before the next layer of batter is poured over it, or simply use a cake tester. If it isn't, bake longer. Pour the same amount of the second batter over the first and bake about the same amount of time.

Continue alternating until all the batter is used or the cake pan is full. When finished, cover with aluminum foil and cool 30 minutes. If desired, sift confectioners' sugar on top. Remove the outer band from the Springform pan. If desired, trim outer edge to showcase the layers. Traditionally, it is served in small pieces with strong coffee.

Original Source: CakiesHQ.com (Spekkoek – Thousand Layer Cake)

19. BONUS RECIPES

Never, ever <u>eat anything in this chapter, especially if it contains essential oils, many of which cannot be ingested.</u> It is also important to store essential oils where children can't reach them.

When people think about cooking, food comes to mind first, for obvious reasons. There are many other good and useful things you can make in the kitchen, although they aren't what most people think of as cooking (or even recipes). When you have allergy problems, even simple things can cause a reaction. Deodorant, sugar scrubs, wipes, and bug repellant are just a few items most households use but most people don't realize can be made cheaply and easily at home. Specialty storage containers, including deodorant containers, are readily available online and in some craft stores.

Many of these recipes use essential oils, especially anti-bacterial ones. The best anti-bacterial essential oils include eucalyptus, lavender, oregano, peppermint, tea tree, and thyme. Each is best suited for specific things, so please do your research before using them, especially if you may use them daily (such as in deodorant). Some studies show tea tree oil and lavender can mimic hormones, for example.

If you want to try homemade sunscreen, the website "Don't Waste The Crumbs" has a post "Homemade Sunscreen with Just 3 Simple Ingredients". It does a great job of explaining how to make it and includes a lot of variations, including different SPFs. If you want more information, read "The Truth About Homemade Sunscreen" on HomemadeToast.com. (Spoiler: The writer strongly believes homemade sunscreen is best.)

Anti-Bacterial Wipes

This was possibly the most surprising thing I made to my family. They couldn't understand why I chose to make wipes when we already had them in the house. But I did it anyway.

8 oz. lotion

8 oz. rubbing alcohol

8 drops essential oil

Ziploc bags

Heavy duty paper towels

Combine equal parts homemade lotion and rubbing alcohol with whatever essential oil you prefer in a glass bowl. (Metal can react and plastic may absorb essential oils, many of which are inedible or even toxic.) While the oils can be any combination you like, make sure at least one has strong anti-bacterial properties, such as lavender or tea tree. There is a partial list in the introduction to this chapter or search online for more detailed information. The wipes should also smell good so it's fine to add popular scents like lemon or orange. The mixture may need to be kneaded.

If the paper towels are larger than you want your wipes, cut them into the size you prefer. Put the paper towels in a sealable bag or container and pour the lotion/alcohol mixture in. Flip the container around as needed to ensure the towels are fully saturated. They should soak up all the liquid within about half an hour. If there is excess liquid, add enough additional paper towels to soak it up. Keep finished wipes in a sealable container or bag.

Original Source: PreparednessMama.com (Homemade Anti-bacterial Wipes)

Bug Repellent

I love essential oils but since my allergies spun out of control, they make me nervous. This is an all-natural bug spray that doesn't use essential oils. When I made it, I put a small strainer on a funnel on a bottle to store it. I poured the mixture straight from the pot into the strainer and funnel. Then I poured the alcohol over it and pressed all the remaining juice out and down the funnel.

> 2 Tbsp. fresh mint
>
> 6 tsp. catnip, citronella, lavender, or cloves

Finely chop the mint and herbs.

> 1 c. water

Boil water, then remove the pot from heat. Add herbs, cover, and cool completely. When it is cool, strain to remove the herbs and squeeze the excess water from the herbs back into the pot.

> 1 c. watch hazel, rubbing alcohol, or vodka

Add witch hazel or alcohol, then pour into a storage container, preferably glass. Store in the refrigerator.

Original Source: DontWasteTheCrumbs.com (Homemade Bug Spray - No Essential Oils)

Cold Pack

This is fantastically simple and cheap. I've made it with Scouts and the kids thought it was fantastic.

> 1 part rubbing alcohol
>
> 3 parts water

Mix and put in a sealed plastic bag in the freezer.

Deodorant

This works better than store-bought brands for me, particularly combined with the sugar scrub.

> ¼ c. arrowroot powder (corn starch works almost as well)

½ c. baking soda

Mix dry ingredients.

6 – 8 Tbsp. coconut oil (solid state)

Add coconut oil gradually until it is smooth and well blended. The texture should be similar to commercial deodorant, soft enough to go on easily but firm enough to hold its shape.

10 drops anti-bacterial essential oil

Add a few drops of essential oil for scent and/or anti-bacterial properties. Since deodorant is used daily, be sure to check for any possible side-effects of long-term use for any essential oil you add. Some studies show tea tree oil and lavender can mimic hormones.

This deodorant melts quickly on warm skin. It also melts quickly on warm days, so use care if you pack it for a trip or you might end with deodorant/coconut oil on everything.

Fragrant Home

The simple reality is that everyone's home smells less than great sometimes. It may just smell of nothing when you want it to smell yummy for guests or it may smell bad from painting, a leaking garbage bag, or a burnt dinner. This is a quick fix. It's also a great way to use leftover herbs, extracts, or citrus fruit.

2 c. water

Boil water.

1 thinly sliced lemon or ¼ c. lemon juice

3 sprigs rosemary

1 Tbsp. vanilla

1 Tbsp. orange zest or extract

Add remaining ingredients. Simmer, adding water as needed. If you (like me) don't read the recipe properly the first time around and already have everything in the pot before boiling the water, heat the water on a lower temperature, then simmer.

Hand Sanitizer (Moisturizing)

I enjoy being able to have a scent I like. Working as a Santa's Elf, I also like being able to add a bit of extra anti-bacterial protection to my hand sanitizer.

> 5-10 drops lavender essential oil
>
> 30 drops tea tree essential oil
>
> 1 Tbsp. witch hazel or vodka
>
> 8 oz. 100% pure aloe vera
>
> ¼ tsp. Vitamin E oil

Combine essential oils and vitamin E in a glass bowl. (Metal can react with the oils and plastic may absorb them.) Add witch hazel or vodka. Combine with aloe vera. Pour it into squirt bottles, pump bottles, or whatever suits your intended use.

Vitamin E is a natural preservative that increases shelf life while softening hands. Light degrades essential oils so store them in dark bottles or a dark place.

Original Source: DIYNatural.com (Natural Moisturizing Hand Sanitizer)

Lavender Spray

This can be used on linens to help with relaxation and sleep, or to help keep moths away. My son inherited some wool uniforms and uses this to keep them safe from moths. When he needs more, he just checks Mom's Cookbook for the recipe.

> 2 Tbsp. (1 oz.) witch hazel or vodka
>
> 10 drops lavender essential oil
>
> 6 Tbsp. (3 oz.) water, preferably distilled

Combine ingredients and mix very well, preferably by shaking in a lidded jar. Pour into a spray bottle. The essential oil won't combine with water by itself. Witch hazel or vodka helps ensure it is more evenly distributed. Glass bottles are better for storage, especially longer-term, because they don't absorb essential oils.

Sugar Scrub

This costs pennies on the dollar compared to buying sugar scrubs at the store and it's super simple to personalize the scent. Truthfully, I have often used the ends of a bottle of canola or other oil that I just wanted to use up and get out of the pantry for this. White sugar works just fine, too.

  2 c. brown sugar

  1 c. of granulated sugar

  1 c. sunflower or other oil

  1 Tbsp. vanilla

Mix the sugars together until there are no lumps. Add sunflower oil and vanilla. You can use different oil but sunflower oil does not have a strong scent like other oils may. Store in a sealed container.

20. MODIFYING AND CREATING RECIPES

I t's time to try modifying your old favorites and finding some ones. Like most things, the first attempt is the hardest. You just need to keep at it until you get the hang of it. Here are the steps that helped me modify the recipes in this book and create new ones.

Simplify, simplify, simplify. The fewer ingredients, the less chance you will react to something. As you are able, you can choose to add more ingredients back in, if you still think you need them. For example, many recipes call for several kinds of cheese. Substitute one young cheese that you can tolerate for all the kinds of cheese as you are starting out and add the other cheeses back, one at a time, as you are able. Maybe you will end up with four different kinds of cheese, but maybe you'll be content with two kinds.

Pesto normally includes pine nuts but the simple recipe here got raves without them. The simplified recipe is perfect.

Substitute something you can have for problematic ingredients. You can often substitute honey for sugar. I sought out the matzo stuffing recipe included in this book for Thanksgiving. You simply can't have stuffing without some kind of bread, and matzo is unleavened bread, making it more compliant. I also regularly substitute ginger for other spices because it's one of the few I can have.

Reimagine it. Salsa is best known as a tomato-based food but there are other kinds, such as peach salsa, that don't contain tomatoes at all. (This is how Seaweed Soup became Seaweed Salad.) Chutney can be used in place of salsa.

Skip or change the condiments/sauce. Tomatoes and tomato sauce are a no-go but some recipes can be compliant by simply using olive oil or a different sauce (white, pesto, etc.) instead. With other meals, changing the sauce can change the entire meal. Sweet and sour sauce on pulled chicken in place of barbeque, for example.

Remove it. Spices are simple to remove from recipes, like onion-free salsa. It can be surprisingly easy to remove ingredients in a lot of recipes, although that is not true with baked goods.

Minimize it. There are many recipes where you can decrease the amount used for problematic ingredients (and with sugar), even if you can't entirely remove it. Many of these recipes have less sugar than the original recipe called for. This helps keep your overall allergen and histamine levels lower. Every little bit helps!

Try new tools. Slow cookers/Crockpots™ are your friend. Use one. So is a sous vide. I've found myself using a small kitchen scale a lot, and I've always used whisks a ton. Because freshly ground meat is better and ground chicken is hard to find (and more compliant), I have a meat grinder now. While some of these tools are a bit pricey, I can't really eat out any more, so I don't feel guilty for buying them.

My most-used tools (beyond the standard basics) include whisks, mortar and pestle, stick blender, kitchen scale, and a sturdy pastry blender.

Remove spices. This is redundant but it bears repeating.

Eating out is tough, no way around it, and you'll probably have to ask for changes to menu items. Most restaurant food has a long list of ingredients. If everything is made from scratch, you can probably get a simplified version of something on the menu, but it's common for restaurants to use at least some pre-made ingredients to speed up the process. At an anniversary dinner, I ordered "toasted gnocchi with roasted garlic, sautéed mushrooms, Italian sausage, and roasted red peppers" without the mushrooms, sausage, and garlic, and with plain, un-infused olive oil instead of the normal infused oil. Another time, I had grilled cheese without the tomato, lettuce, etc. Having to order everything special and different gets old quickly, but it's worth it to stay healthy. If there is something commonly available that you can eat, like plain bread with olive oil for dipping (something I often have), at least you'll have something.

It may take a few minutes studying the menu and you may feel a bit like Sally ordering in *When Harry Met Sally*. I know I do. (Google™ it if you don't know what I'm talking about.) But it's okay. You have to do what you have to do. This is about your health, not about what the waiter or cook or anyone else thinks.

Finally, **mix and match** foods and sauces to make something new. I made "Chicken Breasts", cut them into pieces, and added it to the white sauce and couscous (pasta) for a nice dinner. Half or less of a chicken breast left with fried rice is a full meal. I've marinated meat with different sauces, then cooked them in a stir fry with leftover veggies. When I accidentally defrosted cheese sauce, I added refried beans and made burritos topped with chutney.

A year ago, I doubt I could have done most of the things I talk about in this chapter. As a long-time onion hater, I'm used to leaving some ingredients out of recipes, but I also lacked the experience to be confident in mixing and matching to create new recipes. The new recipes I make are still very basic but my desire to use up leftovers has improved my improvising skills. If this feels overwhelming, just take it one step at a time.

There isn't much risk taking the last ½ c. of sauce and ⅓ of a chicken breast to top a pizza and see how it turns out, or stir-frying them together with the half a carrot and unused ¼ can of peas from yesterday. Worst case, some food that would have been thrown out is thrown out if it turns out badly. Best case, you have a new meal and actually use leftovers before they go bad. When I made the Flax Fried Rice recipe, I actually did use the last parts of a chicken breast I made with my sous vide plus some peas and carrots I didn't use two days earlier. If I hadn't, there's a good chance the chicken, peas, and carrots would have ended up in the garbage.

The pesto sauce as pizza topping was a bit of a disaster because it had too much oil and basically fried the whole thing so it was crispy and not tasty when I took it out, but I still learned from it. The roasted red pepper sauce tasted much better but I can't eat tons of nightshades, so the cheesy white sauce remains my first choice pizza sauce. As you start to experiment, you will find what works best for you. Hopefully the recipes in this book have/will help you enjoy eating, even with the restrictions of an OAS/low histamine diet.

21. Emergency Menu Plans

Between physical and emotional stress, after I have a bad reaction to food, it's hard to remember exactly what I can safely eat that won't stress me out physically or emotionally, and my family certainly can't read my mind and figure it out. It's much easier to create menus for when this happens while we are feeling well because, unfortunately, despite our best efforts, it probably will happen again at some point. If you create "emergency" menu plans for yourself and put them somewhere your family can see/find them, then your family can help when you need it.

Based on my personal experience and nothing more than that, there are two different menus I recommend creating. One is a "Day One" menu for immediately after you react, when it's hard to convince yourself that it's safe to eat anything but you know you need to. Your goal with that menu is simple: food that has nutritional merit that you 100% KNOW you have eaten safely many times, preferably at least once after a previous reaction, and won't react to. The fewer the ingredients it contains, the better. The Week One menu is for the week or even two after a bad reaction and should include as many food groups as you can manage.

My Day One foods are hard boiled eggs, cottage cheese, oatmeal, and saltines. There are a ton more foods I know I can eat without reacting, but the reality is that for the first day or two, I am physically stressed and usually mentally worn out. It's the allergy-equivalent of sick-people food. When we have a cold/flu, most of us want saltines, soup, gelatin, and other easily-digested foods and gradually return to a more balanced diet over a few days. I know it's a similar process for me when I have an allergic reaction to food and I have heard other people say it is similar for them. So, go as basic as you need to but skip the junk food. Your body needs all the help it can get.

I *may* drink Ginger Ale on Day One but that's a pretty big stretch for the first few days, even if I have an upset stomach. I usually end up opening a can and drinking about a tablespoon before getting stressed that I'm reacting and dumping it. I mostly stick to water. Hard-boiled eggs, cottage cheese, and saltines are all things I have eaten after a reaction before on multiple occasions and not only had zero reactions but they have caused me no stress. I can also eat oatmeal but tend to forget about it. If you look at them, three of my four Day One foods are very close to one ingredient. They are easy for me to digest, represent different food groups, and include protein, so I'm content with this, as long as I remember to include the oatmeal for fiber. Previous experiences of only eating dairy and eggs for several days have driven home the critical need to add fiber to my post-reaction diet.

For a Week One menu, stick with simple meals as your body continues to heal and calm down. As an example, I 100% know I can drink Dr. Pepper®, but every time I react to something, drinking it stresses me out and I feel like I'm on the edge of reacting until I get at least two weeks out, and often closer to a full month. There is no point in drinking Dr. Pepper until then. I have much better luck with Ginger Ale and lemon lime sodas which, not coincidentally, also have far fewer ingredients. I also have a harder time with nightshades.

Make a list of the major food groups. Try to have something from each of them in your Week One meal plan, and work really hard to ensure you have fiber or something else to keep your bowels moving properly. It's far too easy to get way off track and have problems from only eating one or two food groups. Of course, your meal plan will be based around your own dietary limitations. If you are allergic to dairy, include your normal dairy substitute is, for example. After you use it, note your reactions and tweak it for the future.

Dairy

While I usually don't eat much yogurt because it is a potential histamine issue, I will eat it after I have a reaction because it is a simple food and because I can easily add granola (fiber), jam (fruit), and other things to make it more interesting as I feel better. Vanilla milkshakes are one of the few things I can normally eat at fast food restaurants, so I often have these (and vanilla ice cream) fairly soon after a reaction.

Fruit

Honestly, I'll be fine going a few weeks without fruit – and I will for a few weeks after a reaction. I may, however, eat berry compote or a berry pie, or some jam on toast or mixed into yogurt.

Grain

A demi-loaf of French bread from one particular local grocery store dipped in olive oil is one of my go-to foods when I'm having a hard time and, honestly, could be one of my Day One meals, except going out to the grocery store is usually more than I want to do then. I can also eat grilled cheese, oatmeal, and simple pasta meals

Protein

Chicken breasts, pulled chicken with no sauce, egg salad (just eggs and cream cheese), and roasted chickpeas are all protein-rich options I can enjoy, even shortly after a reaction. Personally, I find that it takes me longer to return to "normal" if I don't have some protein every day.

Vegetables

I can eat any of the roasted vegetables in this cookbook even in the week after a reaction but I have to avoid nightshades, including ones I normally eat, for at least a week or two after a bad reaction. Sadly, that includes potato chips. Of course, having the energy and desire to make roasted vegetables is an entirely different story and I rarely have that energy in the aftermath of a bad reaction.

Soups are much easier to make and digest, but the only one I usually have the stamina to make is matzo ball, in part because you make part of it, then have a break while it's in the refrigerator before finishing it.

Snacks

I struggle with how many things we are told are healthy that aren't healthy *for me*. Chocolate is one of those foods. The darker it is, the worse it is for me and the longer I have to wait after a reaction to eat it again. Roasted chickpeas are one of the first snacks I can start eating again.

There are a lot of other foods I 100% know I can eat (or drink, like Ginger Ale), but that stress me out for the first week or two. I gradually add them back in as my body calms back down. Most of us have friends and family who want to help when we are struggling, no matter what the struggle. Making Day One and Week One menus and posting them where they can find them–like on the side of the refrigerator–is a good way to help them help us after an allergic reaction. It's also a good way to help ourselves because it's a reminder of what we can/should be eating for when we really need it and have a hard time remembering.

I frequently get myself into trouble by having almost nothing except eggs and dairy for most of the first week after a reaction because it's very easy to stick with those Day One foods. However, it always leads to intestinal issues. Avoiding those is my primary incentive for creating a Week One menu. I don't want to go there *again!* Simply remembering to regularly add in oatmeal will go a long way toward relieving the distress I routinely feel starting a few days after a reaction since it is caused entirely by an out of whack diet.

Now it's your turn. Create a Day One menu for yourself, then a Week One menu. Double-check your Week One menu to make sure you have more than one food group. Print them out and put them somewhere you and your family/friends can find them easily.

Appendix 1: Additional Low Histamine Resources

I like kids' cookbooks because the recipes are simpler and they often try to hide fruits and veggies in other foods, which also means they are well-cooked. ***Deceptively Delicious* by Jessica Seinfeld (Jerry's wife) uses tons of pureed veggies. *Betty Crocker's Lost Recipes* has a ton of great, simple options.** If you only buy one other cookbook, make it one of those. There aren't any recipes from either of these in this book because those recipes didn't need modified, and all the recipes included in this book were modified to some extent. After you buy/order one of those, please browse around some of the source sites for recipes you liked in this book.

Cooking methods can greatly impact histamine levels. Both old-school slow cookers and newly-popular sous vide are good ways to help ensure food is thoroughly cooked and to reduce how much time you have to spend watching it cook. Sous vide recipes are widely available online, and slow cooker cookbooks are everywhere, including Grandma's kitchen and used bookstores. There can be a lot of prep for the recipes, but in the end, you get to leave while they cook instead of standing over the stove the whole time. That's a win in my book.

Recipe Sources

AllRecipes.com and the *All Recipes* magazine

Crockpot/slow cooker cookbooks (especially for OAS issues)

Kids' cookbooks

Low histamine websites—Many have one or more cookbooks for low histamine cooking, although I didn't see any that also address OAS.

Paleo AIP Recipe Roundtables:
   www.phoenixhelix.com/paleo-aip-recipe-roundtables

Allergy Free Cookbook

Betty Crocker's Lost Recipes

Cooking with ___ Ingredients series (4, 5, etc.)

Dad's Book of Awesome Recipes by Mike Adamick

Deceptively Delicious by **Jessica Seinfeld**

The Moms' Guide to Meal Makeovers by Janice Bissex and Liz Weiss

The Quaker Oats Cookbook (especially if you need more fiber)

Getting Started

Alison Vickery: Books, anti-histamine food lists, and more.
www.alisonvickery.com.au/anti-histamine-foods

**Swiss Interest Group Histamine Intolerance Food List. Google
"SIGHI Food List", print it, and use it.** (This Swiss site is a great
resource but they are still translating some pages into English.)
**www.mastzellaktivierung.info/downloads/foodlist/21_FoodList_E
N_alphabetic_withCateg.pdf**

Easy Protein Swaps to Lower Amines
www.alisonvickery.com.au/easy-protein-swaps-that-lower-amines-
without-cutting-foods

Healing Histamine: Tons of information, books, and courses.
www.healinghistamine.com

Low Histamine Ingredient Substitutions
www.women.com/shannon/lists/low-histamine-ingredient-substitutions

Nightshades: Reasons for Eliminating Them
www.thepaleomom.com/the-whys-behind-autoimmune-protocol

Therapy for Histamine Intolerance
www.frusano.com/en/intolerances/histamine-intolerance/therapy-for-
histamine-intolerance.html

What is Oral Allergy Syndrome?
www.healthline.com/health/oral-allergy-syndrome

APPENDIX 2: SPECIFIC TOPICS

There is no way one book can contain all the information on cooking or food allergies. These links are to articles that helped me improve my cooking, understand ingredients, or understand allergy/histamine issues better. They have helped me improve my health and I think they can help you too.

In the course of writing this book, I found myself coming back to the website "The Spruce Eats" time and again for recipes and cooking advice. As a result, there are more than a few links here to that website and I recommend referring back to them and just surfing their website to help hone your cooking skills.

Allergy and Histamine Issues

Celery Allergy
www.anaphylaxis.org.uk/wp-content/uploads/2015/06/Celery-version-9-formatted-with-changes-to-terminology-re-pollen-food.pdf
www.whatallergy.com/2011/04/celeryallergy

DAO Blocking Foods
www.mindbodygreen.com/0-11175/everything-you-need-to-know-about-histamine-intolerance.html

Effects of Cooking on Histamine Levels in Selected Foods
www.ncbi.nlm.nih.gov/pmc/articles/PMC5705351

Hidden Gluten, Grains and Nightshades in Meds and Supplements
www.autoimmunewellness.com/hidden-gluten-grains-and-nightshades-in-meds-and-supplements

High DAO Foods
www.alisonvickery.com.au/why-olive-oil-and-a-paleo-diet-increases-dao
www.healinghistamine.com/dr-joneja-how-to-boost-your-histamine-lowering-dao-enzyme-naturally

www.jillcarnahan.com/2018/03/19/boost-your-dao-levels-to-fight-histamine

Low Histamine Substitutions
www.women.com/shannon/lists/low-histamine-ingredient-substitutions

Menopause Histamine Connection
themenopausehistamineconnection.wordpress.com

Nightshade Free Survival Guide
www.phoenixhelix.com/2013/06/23/nightshade-free-survival-guide

Nutrient Deficiencies and Histamine Intolerance
factvsfitness.com/nutrient-deficiencies-histamine-intolerance/

Quercetin Food Chart (a natural antihistamine)
www.quercetin.com/overview/food-chart

Wine Histamine Levels
www.factvsfitness.com/low-histamine-wine
www.finewineandgoodspirits.com/wcsstore/WineandSpirits/learnentertain /entertain/wine_sensitivities.html

The Wine Wand: Histamine and Sulfite Filter
drinkpurewine.com

Cooking/Recipes

Candy Bar Recipes
www.thespruceeats.com/candy-bar-recipes-521265

Cooking with Peanut Powder
www.epicurious.com/ingredients/how-to-cook-with-powdered-peanut-butter-recipes-tips-article

Different Kinds of Salt
www.sheknows.com/food-and-recipes/articles/1140764/types-of-salt

Five Mother Sauces Every Cook Should Know
food52.com/blog/12209-the-five-mother-sauces-every-cook-should-know
www.finedininglovers.com/blog/food-drinks/mother-sauces-recipes
www.thespruceeats.com/mother-sauces-996119

SPECIFIC TOPICS

Flavored Salt Recipes
www.sheknows.com/food-and-recipes/articles/1107353/flavored-salt-recipes

Flavored Water Recipes (use care: some have potential allergy issues)
www.theyummylife.com/Flavored_Water
www.52kitchenadventures.com/2012/09/17/fifty-awesome-flavored-water-recipes
greatist.com/health/flavored-water-healthy-recipe

Make Your Own Sushi
www.MakeSushi.com
minimalistbaker.com/how-to-make-sushi-without-a-mat

Popcorn (Flavored)
www.tasteofhome.com/collection/flavored-popcorn-recipes
www.swansonvitamins.com/blog/jenessa/diy-popcorn-seasonings

Rice-Free ("Low Carb") Sushi (substitute cream cheese for rice)
www.ditchthecarbs.com/carbs-in-sushi

Swapping Dry Mustard for Prepared Mustard
www.thespruceeats.com/substitute-dry-mustard-for-prepared-mustard-995466

General

Annatto/Cheddar Cheese and its color
www.thespruceeats.com/white-vs-yellow-cheddar-cheese-2355816
www.thespruceeats.com/what-is-achiote-or-annatto-2138265

Every Popular Sweetener Ranked*
www.eatthis.com/sweeteners
*With over 20 sweeteners, it includes some lesser-known ones.

Does It Go Bad?
www.doesitgobad.com

How Imitation Crab Meat is Made
www.madehow.com/Volume-3/Imitation-Crab-Meat.html

How to Drink Sake
www.sakesocial.com/blogs/beau/11418437-how-to-drink-sake

Inhibiting Bacteria Growth in Sushi
sciencenordic.com/inhibiting-bacteria-growth-sushi

Recognizing Good and Bad Olive Oil
www.olivetomato.com/how-to-recognize-good-and-bad-olive-oil

Sake 101: A Beginners Guide to Sake
boutiquejapan.com/sake101

Types of Sake
sake-world.com/about-sake/types-of-sake

APPENDIX 3: COMPLIANT FOODS

These foods are generally compliant, assuming they don't contain additives from the not compliant list. Most are ingredients you can use to make other food. For example, applesauce is compliant but store-bought containers may have cinnamon, or other additives and trace ingredients.

Applesauce

Baking Powder

Baking Soda

Butter

Cheese–ricotta, young
   Gouda, mild cheddar

Chicken

Cookies

Cottage Cheese

Cream Cheese

Cream of Tartar

Cream of Wheat

Eggs

Garlic

Gelatin (plain)

Ginger

Graham Crackers

Gravy (homemade)

Grits

Honey

Jelly/Jam

Lamb

Legumes (except soy
   beans and red beans)

Maple Syrup

Melba toast

Milk (not flavored)

Molasses

Oatmeal

Onion

Pasta

Pie

Puffed Rice and Wheat

Rye Bread

Rye Krisp

Saltines

Seaweed (nori)

Turkey

Vegetable Oil (pure)

Wasa light or golden
   crackers

SIMPLE COOKING FOR ALLERGIES

Alcohol: vodka (if you can eat potatoes), gin, white rum
(That's the complete list of compliant alcohol.)

The link below is to an English translation from a German-language website with information on whether an incredibly long list of food is high histamine, high in other amines, a histamine liberator, or a DAO blocker. It is more thorough and contains more specific details than any other list I found, and this is not the only place you can find this link in this book. (Search for "SIGHI food list" so you don't have to copy the link; this is not the only place I have included it in this book.)

www.mastzellaktivierung.info/downloads/foodlist/21_FoodList_EN
_alphabetic_withCateg.pdf

APPENDIX 4: YOUR TOLERATED FOODS

As you gradually add new foods, use this Appendix and the following one to note foods you can and cannot tolerate. This Appendix focuses on common foods and notes specific cross-reactors for OAS. An * indicates foods known to potentially cause histamine problems in at least one area. This can be a reference list of what you can eat, separate from your food diary.

Fruits

Apple (tree, mugwort)

Apricot (tree)

Bananas (ragweed)

Berries

    Blackberry
    Blueberry
    Cranberry
    Raspberry
    *Strawberry (tree)

Cherry (tree)

Date (grass)

Fig (tree, grass)

Grape

Guava

Key lime

Kiwi (tree, grass)

*Lemon

*Lime

Lychee (tree)

Mango

Melons (grass, ragweed, mugwort)

    Cantaloupe
    Honeydew
    Watermelon (grass, ragweed, mugwort)

Nectarine (tree)

*Orange (grass, mugwort)

Peach (tree, mugwort)

Pear (tree)

Persimmon (tree)

Plantain

Plum (tree)

Pomegranate

Prune (tree)

General

Annatto (a common additive)

Applesauce

Bread

Butter

Cereal

*Chocolate
  *Cocoa (powder)
  *Dark
  *Milk
  White

Corn

Corn meal

Corn syrup

Cottage cheese

Cream cheese

Eggs

Flour
  Almond
  Oat
  Rice
  Rye
  Wheat

Honey

Lentils (tree)

Milk

Molasses

Mustard

Oats/Oatmeal

Peanuts (tree, grass)

Peanut butter

Pretzels
  Hard
  Soft

Ricotta

*Sour cream

*Soy sauce

*Soybean (tree)

*Sunflower seeds (tree, mugwort)

*Teriyaki sauce

*Tree nuts (tree)
  Almond (tree)
  Coconut
  Hazelnut (tree)
  Macadamia
  Pine nut
  Walnut (tree)

Vanilla

*Yeast/leavening

*Yogurt
  *Plain
  *Greek

Meat/Poultry

*Bacon

*Beef

*Bologna

Chicken

Deer/Venison

Duck

Lamb

Pork

Turkey

*Salami and deli meat

Nightshades (a family of fruits and vegetables)

All nightshades are a potential histamine problem.

*Eggplants/aubergines

*Goji berries

*Peppers – including flakes

    *Bell peppers
    *Cayenne peppers
    *Chili peppers
    *Jalapenos)
    *Red peppers
    *Sweet peppers

*Pimentos

*Potato (tree, grass)

*Potatoes – potato starch

* (Nightshade) Spices

    *Chili powder
    *Chinese 5-Spice Powder
    *Curry Powder
    *Hot Sauce
    *Paprika

*Tamarillos

*Tomatillos

*Tomato (tree, grass, mugwort)

Sweeteners

Agave Syrup

Aspartame

Corn Syrup

Honey

Maple Syrup

Molasses

Saccharin

Sorbitol

Splenda

Stevia

Sugar
    Brown
    Cane

Confectioners/powdered
White

Xylitol

Vegetables

*Avocado

Beans (tree)

Broccoli (mugwort)

Cabbage (mugwort)

Carrot (tree, mugwort)

Cauliflower (mugwort)

Celery (tree, mugwort)

Chard (mugwort)

Cucumbers (ragweed)

Lettuce
  Bibb
  Iceberg
  Red Leaf
  Romaine

Onion (mugwort)

Red
White

Parsnip (tree, mugwort)

Peas (tree, grass)

*Peppers
  Bell (sweet peppers are compliant) (mugwort)
    *Chili
    *Green (tree, mugwort)
    *Jalapeno
    *Red

*Spinach

Squash

Sweet potatoes/yams

Zucchini (ragweed)

APPENDIX 5: YOUR TOLERATED HERBS AND SPICES

For me, the blandness of my initial diet was even harder than the limited number of foods. I miss spices! Unlike fruits and vegetables, **cooking *does not* necessarily make spices less reactive** so be very careful and methodical as you add these back into your diet, and continue avoiding the generic "spices." And as much as it truly sucks, some (or many) spices may permanently be gone from your diet.

More than a year after my initial reaction, I have a handful of spices and herbs I know I can eat, but it really isn't worth the risk to try more very often. I have reacted to quite a few. While my family knows to add spices to anything I make, I have learned to be content with just my handful of spices. It's worth it to not have heart palpitations and all the other problems that have resolved with the reduction in allergens.

Using dried herbs instead of fresh can reduce reactivity but remain cautious, as with other foods you reintroduce.

Herbs

Basil

Bay leaves

Borage

Caraway

Chamomile

Chives

Cilantro

Dill

Elderflower/Elderberry

Fennel

Garlic (mugwort)
  Fresh
  Powder

Gingko Biloba

Ginseng

Hibiscus

Horseradish

Lavender

Lemon Balm

Lemongrass

Lemon Verbena

Lemon Zest

Licorice root (not the candy)

Marjoram

Mint/Spearmint/Peppermint

Mugwort (mugwort)

Mustard seed

Nigella

Onion (mugwort)
    Fresh

Powder
Shallot

Oregano (tree, mugwort)

Parsley

Poppy seed

Rosemary

Saffron

Sage

Sesame seed

Tarragon

Thyme (tree)

Watercress

Spices

Allspice

Anise seed (mugwort)

Cajun Seasoning

Caraway (mugwort)

Cardamom

Cayenne pepper

Celery seed/salt

Chili powder

Chinese Five Spice

Cinnamon

Cloves

Coriander (mugwort)

Cumin (mugwort)

Curry

Fennel (mugwort)

Garam masala

Ginger
    Fresh
    Powder

Jerk seasoning

Mace

Mustard

Nigella

YOUR TOLERATED HERBS AND SPICES

Nutmeg

Paprika

Pepper (black) (mugwort)

Pepper (white)

Red pepper

Saffron

Star Anise

Tabasco

Tiki masala

Turmeric

Vanilla

Wasabi

INDEX

ABOUT THE AUTHOR

Bethanne Kim was allergy free for most of her life, until she wasn't. She went to the allergist after onions started making her nauseous and was shocked to learn that she was highly allergic to most of nature and had allergy-induced asthma that was raging completely and utterly out of control. (In retrospect, that did explain the difficulty she had been having breathing.) On one test (FeNO), she had the worst score her allergist had ever seen: nearly 4 times the "bad" level.

A few years later, she developed Oral Allergy Syndrome and a variety of other food allergies. Like most people with bad allergies, this led her to learning more about allergies and taking a lot of medications. Since she's not the only one in her extended family with allergies, Thanksgiving is a particular challenge. Wheat, corn, nuts, garlic, onions, spices, and more must be avoided for the extended family. It's not easy! The key is to remember that everyone needs to eat, but they don't need to be able to eat every single dish.

She chose to publish this cookbook to help others, but the main impetus was making sure she had food she could safely eat and enjoy. Between this and her other cookbook

Kim is a wife and the mother of two. Like too many families, cooking for everyone's dietary issues can be a challenge, but it's one she's determined to meet with the help of the recipes in this book.

OTHER BOOKS

The Constitution: It's the OS for the US explains the historical context for the US Constitution and describes how it works using computer terms like firewall and plug-ins, not legalese. (An OS is a computer Operating System, like iOS for Apple devices.)

Survival Skills for All Ages Book 1: Basic Life Skills covers skills so simple most emergency preparedness books skip right over them. In true emergencies, knowing how to sharpen kitchen knives and basic sanitation can be literal life savers. Skills were chosen for their value in everyday life as well as emergencies.

Survival Skills for All Ages Book 2: 26 Mental & Urban Life Skills covers financial skills, staying safe while traveling, self-defense, cyber security, hiding from danger, handling your emotions (including stress and anger), and more. These skills can help kids and adults throughout life, not just in emergencies.

Survival Skills for All Ages Book 3: Simple Cooking for Families is full of simple recipes that can be cooked using long-term storage ingredients and basic farm produce (fresh dairy and eggs), and recipes for staples such as mayonnaise, baking powder, sweetened condensed milk, and crackers. It also talks about the tools you need to cook without power.

Survival Skills for All Ages Book 4: Simple Cooking for Allergies: Oral Allergy Syndrome and Low Histamine Food explains what foods are low histamine, why others are high histamine, and how to eat a low histamine diet while also avoiding the uncooked fruits and veggies that can cause problems for oral allergy syndrome sufferers. There is information on how to modify your

own favorite recipes and where to find more information as you move forward and add new foods to your diet.

Cubmastering: Getting Started as Cubmaster is an introduction for new Cubmasters. Topics covered include organizational structure, training, recruiting, and recharter. This is about more than just the nuts and bolts of Scouting, though. It also covers dealing with difficult parents and planning special pack events.

Scout Leader: An Introduction to Boy Scouts focuses on the nuts and bolts of the Boy Scouts of America with particular emphasis on how units in Cub Scouts and Scouts BSA are supposed to work. Recharter, training, common BSA meetings (such as Roundtable), and much more are described. Each chapter starts with a quote from Lord Baden Powell.

Citizenship in the World: Teaching the Merit Badge is, quite simply, a guide to assist merit badge counselors in teaching the BSA Eagle-required merit badge "Citizenship in the World." It includes the merit badge requirements, and information and tips for teaching it.

The Organized Wedding: Planning Everything from Your Engagement to Your Marriage is chock full of checklists. No detail is too small! What truly sets it apart is including the actual wedding ceremony and a chapter on your marriage with questions on financial priorities, family health history, and all your doctors.

OMG! Not the Zombies! Book 1 A group of teens goes for a hike and accidentally starts the zombie apocalypse. They start setting up a safe community in some old Indian cliff houses and stocking it with supplies to save their families and themselves while the adults are still pretending life is normal.

OTHER BOOKS

BRB! Not the Zombies! Book 2 As their group grows, they discover a new mission: Get crucial information and items to the CDC to help with efforts to create a cure for the Infection. They fight their way through zombie-infested towns to reach the "impregnable" CDC research station their hopes are pinned on.

YOLO! Not the Zombies! Book 3 Have you ever wondered how a hurricane might affect the zombie apocalypse? Or how undead would fare in a sandstorm? (Hint: Hope they aren't wearing a helmet.) These and other natural disasters are explored in these zombie short stories.

Works in Progress:

Survival Skills for All Ages: 26 Outdoor Life Skills covers basic camping skills such as knot tying, fire building, outdoor cooking, and choosing a tent. It also covers hunting, fishing, and foraging for food; finding your way using maps, compasses, and GPSs; and truly basic skills such as managing time and water safety (tides, currents, etc.).

Survival Skills for All Ages: Special Needs Prepping may sound like something only "other people" need but the truth is that most families have special needs. Babies, elderly parents, diabetes, asthma, allergies–most of us have at least one of these and even if we don't, a simple sprained ankle or back injury can make us (temporarily) special needs.

Scouting in the Deep End: Association with Adults

CONTACT THE AUTHOR

Bethanne Kim would love to hear from you! You can connect with her through:

Email: Bethanne@BethanneKim.com

Blog: BethanneKim.com

Facebook: BethanneKim

Pinterest: BethanneKim

Twitter: @Bethanne_Kim

Instagram: BethanneKim

Because Amazon reviews really do matter, especially for indie authors, please take a few minutes and post a review of this book on Amazon.com.

www.ingramcontent.com/pod-product-compliance
Lightning Source LLC
Chambersburg PA
CBHW051419090426
42737CB00014B/2737